REVIEWERS AGREE: MARY HUNT MAKES MONEY WORK FOR YOU!

"Hunt has become so competent at pinching pennies that she teaches others the fine art through *The Cheapskate Monthly*."
—*Business Week*

"Her straightforward advice ranges on subjects from coupons and discount shopping to insurance policies . . . Hunt's upbeat attitude doesn't come across as a lecture, and she makes it clear she's not denying herself simple pleasures."
—*Los Angeles Times*

"*The Cheapskate Monthly* is filled with humorous first-person stories, reader mail and advice."
—*Orange County Register*

St. Martin's Paperbacks titles
by Mary Hunt

THE BEST OF THE CHEAPSKATE MONTHLY

THE CHEAPSKATE MONTHLY
MONEY MAKEOVER

The CHEAP-SKATE MONTHLY

MONEY MAKEOVER

MARY HUNT

ST. MARTIN'S PAPERBACKS

The Norman Vincent Peale passage on pp. 99–101 is quoted with permission from *Plus* magazine, Vol. 40/No. 4 (Part III), May 1989. Copyright © 1989 by Foundation for Christian Living, P.O. Box FCL, Pawling, NY 12564, (914) 855-5000.

THE CHEAPSKATE MONTHLY MONEY MAKEOVER

ISBN: 0-312-95411-5

Printed in the United States of America

St. Martin's Paperbacks edition/March 1995

10 9 8 7 6 5 4 3 2 1

This book is lovingly dedicated to the thousands of people who make up the *Cheapskate Monthly* family. You have encouraged me with your loyalty, strength, and determination. I consider it a privilege to walk the path of financial solvency beside you.

Acknowledgments

I wish to thank personally the thousands of people who have written to me over the past three years. Your candor, courage, and reports of progress have encouraged me more than you will ever know. Your enthusiasm and approval ratings have annihilated my perceived personal limitations and your willingness to share your personal financial struggles and remarkable progress have contributed to the success of *Cheapskate Monthly*. Special thanks to my assistant Cathy Hollenbeck for her constant help, invaluable expertise, and loyal support; Chris Purcell for hours of manuscript reading; my agent Toni Lopopolo; my editor Jennifer Weis and the staff at St. Martin's Press. Finally, I want to acknowledge and thank my wonderful husband Harold and sons Jeremy and Josh for their love and patience, and for never complaining when the table is covered with books and manuscripts instead of dinner.

Table of Contents

Special Notice

The information given in this book is intended to provide you with lay advice on ways and means of overcoming debt and achieving financial solvency. It is not intended as a substitute for sound legal and accounting advice from your attorney or financial advisor.

What follows should be taken as procedural suggestions. Before acting on any of these suggestions you should read them carefully. No two financial situations are exactly alike. Always seek professional advice before making major changes in your financial life.

Anything you attempt to do toward the rapid repayment of any loan must be in agreement with the loan's legal document. The lender, as well as the borrower, has the right to reject any plan which is not specified in the loan agreement.

The information in this book is to the author's knowledge conceptually correct. The mathematics used are based on standard mathematical formulas. The exact numbers may vary from other amortization schedules or formulas because of the way in which numbers are rounded. There also may be a difference because of the way the interest is calculated.

The examples herein are given only to illustrate concepts. Even if they seem to fit your particular circumstances, your lending agreement and attorney's advice will supercede any suggestion I've made.

INTRODUCTION

A terrible thing happened to me several years ago. I got into awful financial trouble. Now when I say awful I don't mean just uncomfortable or that I turned up a few bucks short now and then. I mean awful, embarrassing, bigger-than-life kind of terrible.

It took me a "mere" 12 years to run up enough consumer debt to bankrupt a small country. How that all happened, how we were able to reverse the process, and how we repaid the debt became the subject matter which prompted me to write and publish a subscription newsletter, *Cheapskate Monthly*. From that endeavor came my first book, *The Best of Cheapskate Monthly*, (St. Martin's Paperbacks, 1993), which launched a new and wonderful career. Often I am humbled by the irony that the very topic which nearly ruined us now brings me such joy and fulfillment.

Since giving birth to *Cheapskate Monthly* I have read piles of books, written hundreds of articles, and received thousands of letters. I have shown up on dozens of radio and television talk shows, have been interviewed by scores of reporters, and spent more time than I like to remember on the phone. And I've reached one "brilliant" conclusion after another—not the least of which is this:

1

THE BIGGEST REASON PEOPLE FALL INTO FINANCIAL DIFFICULTY IS THEY DON'T KNOW HOW TO CONTROL THEIR SPENDING.

Simple as that. People who do not control their spending find themselves in a variety of financial difficulties, from just slightly out of balance to contemplating suicide. They are convinced that more money would cure their financial ills. The truth is that their problem has nothing to do with having too little money. The problem is they don't know how to manage what they already have!

Regardless of the level of financial difficulty in which you find yourself, the terror you are feeling right now is very much the same felt by those who are in much less difficulty, or far more. It's like being stranded in the middle of the ocean. It doesn't matter if you are in over your head by two feet or by two thousand feet. Unless you reach for the life preserver you are going down.

Well, have I got a life preserver for you! It's called a Money Makeover. It's not a scam, it won't require that you buy anything and it is not too good to be true. It is the result of analyzing my own situation, looking at hundreds of others' financial plights, talking to thousands of people, figuring out the common problems, and then finding reasonable and logical solutions.

Let me make sure you understand something: I

am not a financial planner, an accountant, attorney, or a certified anything. I am a wife and a mother who got into terrible financial trouble. I limped along, learning a lot along the way. Now I help others who find themselves in similar situations to avoid the things I did wrong while pointing them toward things I did right.

You are going to be ecstatic to discover that in a few relatively painless steps, you could have your finances back in control by next month at this time. (Okay, for some of you that might be stretching it a bit.) One month is enough time to make significant progress. It is more than enough time to make a few major decisions which will determine the entire course of your life from this day on. You won't need to buy any fancy computers, invest in any easy-payment video tape series, or show up at group meetings.

In the following pages through their stories and letters you are going to have the opportunity to meet many people just like yourself. I have chosen to use first names only in order to protect their privacy. Many of these people looked at their situations and instead of sitting around wallowing in self-pity decided to do something to take control of their lives by getting a grip on how they spend their money. I hope through their examples you will find the courage you need to do the same. Some letters will express their frustrations and struggles. Everyone you will meet on the following pages is in process. We are seeking progress, not perfection!

Hopefully by sharing their experiences, strength, successes, and struggles, you will be encouraged to join these courageous individuals on the road to fiscal freedom and financial ease.

Your financial plight may seem so overwhelming to you right now that you find yourself paralyzed. Perhaps the very idea of dealing with your finances is so complicated you don't even know where to start. The purpose of a money makeover is to take a jumbo-sized situation and break it down into manageable parts.

No matter how many times you've tried to conform to a rigid budget, no matter how many times you've failed, now is the time to learn new behaviors which will lead to lifelong change. In the time it takes you to read this book and follow the simple instructions you will be enjoying your new "look," —your Money Makeover!

Mary Hunt
California, 1994

I wrote to you after reading your book, *The Best of Cheapskate Monthly*. At that time I was in serious financial trouble struggling to climb out of a dark pit. I say 'dark' because my situation had thrown me into a major depression robbing me of any feelings of worth I once had. I felt quite entitled to charge clothes, make-up, manicures, and massages on my credit cards to make myself feel better.

I was under the load of a car loan, a student loan, two personal lines of credit, MasterCard and Visa card debts along with several credit cards from department stores. I had phone bills, calling card bills, medical bills, rent, and on and on. I could see no way out and I was, quite literally, a complete mess!

After reading your book I knew you were someone who could identify with me and from whom I could take advice. I want to confirm your strong belief that no matter what the circumstances, NO situation is hopeless. I am living proof. Here are some of the steps I took to empower myself to take control and turn things around.

I called Consumer Credit Counseling Services and set up an appointment. I was afraid to admit I was in a serious predicament and needed help. After all, I am an intelligent individual with a college degree; I should be able to figure this out for myself.

When I finally forced myself to go I was amazed to see other people just like me—intelligent people who'd gone too far with credit. It was not the humiliating experience I expected. CCCS contacted my credit card creditors and in some instances were able to lower the interest rate I was paying. They set up a budget for me and I now pay one low monthly payment to CCCS. I was amazed how much respect I received from my creditors after agreeing to this plan.

I made a visit to my credit union and refinanced my car loan. I have a lower interest rate and now the payment is deducted directly from my paycheck and it's never late. I never see the money so I don't miss it.

I followed your advice and began to save ten percent of my earnings as well as give away 10 percent. These two actions have to be the best anecdote for a rotten self-image. Not only am I helping others I'm helping myself. Eventually as the bills began to decrease I was able to save even more. I can't begin to tell you what a thrill it is to watch my savings grow. It works!

I began to pay off my remaining debts in small increments. Instead of ignoring my obligations like I used to I make small monthly payments and my bills have been reduced significantly.

I started doing things for myself. When I began to save I really became a bona fide cheapskate. I knew that a manicure every week would result in $12 out of my savings. I could be saving $48 a month just by taking the time to give myself a manicure. And since my debt reduction and savings plans were giving me enough satisfaction I no longer needed or desired so many luxuries. I organized all of the luxuries I've been buying over the years. I discovered I have enough make-up to last for a long, long time.

Again I took your advice and joined my company's 401K plan. Even though my employer doesn't match my contribution the funds are taken directly from my paycheck before taxes are taken out. Thus, I never see this money and my taxes at the end of the year are lower! There are benefits to a 401K even if the company doesn't match the contribution.

I live on a cash basis. Giving up the credit cards was not as difficult as I thought it would be. I now pay cash for everything. I have one credit card to use for making hotel reservations or renting a car but it is tied to my checking account so that if I ever use it to make a purchase it will be paid off automatically from my account.

Mary, I know that I don't have far to go until I am debt-free, and I can't wait! Please stress to your readers there is hope. Taking responsibility and doing something about it is so empowering. I feel better about myself and my future than I ever have, and it really shows in my attitude. Patience and perseverance have really paid off for me.

Sarah

CHAPTER 1

I've Been Where You Are

There's a very good chance I've been where you are now, financially speaking. I've experienced just about every situation imaginable. I've been slightly uncomfortable. I've been in huge jams. I've gone through minor dilemmas, moments of unbelievable abundance, and seasons of interminable financial drought. I've been on the mountaintop of plenty, in the valley of desperation and every point between. I've made most of life's worst financial decisions. I know the secret terror of wondering not if, but when, to call the bankruptcy attorney. On more than one occasion I've thrown myself into a heap wailing, "This is it, there's absolutely no way out this time."

From time to time I experienced the delight of having what I considered large sums money come my way. But time and time again to my utter astonishment instead of "more money" solving the problems and fixing everything, I would be left in an even worse situation when the money seemed to disappear into thin air.

I know what it feels like to live in a perpetual financial panic while trying to keep up appearances, dodge creditor's phone calls, figure out clever new ways to make sure the mail mysteriously disappears, hide the shopping bags, cope with foreclosure notices, finagle, contrive, and cleverly deceive. I know how to manage a new outfit even when the checking account is overdrawn, the utilities haven't been paid, and the credit cards are way beyond their limit.

I've been caught up in the trap of worshiping money, convinced that just having enough of it will fix everything. I know how to envy others who in my distorted way of thinking have perfect lives, make more money than God, and are my living proof that money can absolutely buy happiness beyond belief. I know how to zap the joy right out of a marriage. I know how to put a spouse under so much financial pressure that his career is in jeopardy and his patience is all but spent.

Believe me, if financial juggling were an Olympic event I'd be wearing a gold medal.

No matter what shape your finances are in, no matter how embarrassed, frightened, or uneasy you are right now, relax. I know what you are going through. If I haven't experienced your exact situation I probably know someone who has. I've heard it all, so you can't shock me. You should find comfort in knowing you are not alone and relief in understanding I'm not going to judge, condemn, or flog you.

My own excursion into credit hell began quite innocently. As a college freshman I quickly adapted to the privacy, convenience, and freedom my personal checking account offered. And the flexibility—that was the best part. By exercising a few clever maneuvers I could make purchases as early as Wednesday, get paid on Friday, deposit my check the following Monday and feel a little bit too cocky knowing that once again I had beaten the system. No problem. I could appear as affluent as any of my friends. I could cash checks at the local market and have sufficient time to figure out how to cover them later, in private and at a more convenient time.

My propensity to spend money that I didn't actually have was greatly enhanced upon the occasion of my marriage to Harold Hunt. I got my very first credit card! As credit cards go it was no real prize. It was a gasoline card which required full payment each month. It didn't greatly enhance my spending abilities but it did free up cash which heretofore had been required to purchase fuel. And it was certainly superior to our checking account. With the advent of more efficient computer systems the bank had rudely shortened the period of time I had between writing checks and depositing funds to cover them.

It was a time in my life when I experienced the ultimate in mixed emotions. I was proud that Harold had aspired to the position of bank manager, but he was *my* bank manager and so it was becoming increasingly more difficult to hide my audacious activities. With my Texaco credit card I felt quite entitled to "fill 'er up" at will and then enjoy 30 days of denial before being faced with the inevitable pain of payment.

My first credit card kept me happy for oh, two or three months until the gentle beckoning of other credit cards with more potential won me over. I began collecting plastic, not because I had a particular reason or plan but just to have in case of emergency. The problem is that I became a habitual user. I had a lot of emergencies. Plastic spending felt good, too, because it relieved the panic. Plastic was convenient, it was socially acceptable, and it allowed me to enjoy now and worry later.

In time I no longer saw my purchases for their price tag but for what they represented as a monthly payment. A 10 or 15 dollar minimum monthly payment seemed hardly worth a second thought. Such a reasonable payment amounted to mere pennies. Surely we'd never even notice it. I was impressed with the payment arrangement the credit card companies offered. The issue of interest charges never crossed my mind. The all-consuming issue for me was having as many lines of credit with the highest limits possible.

Over the course of the first 12 years of our marriage I managed to do a few remarkable things, not the least of which was give birth. I had two boys we named Jeremy and Josh. So anxious was I to relive my own childhood through the two most wonderful kids on earth that my unbridled spending now had a higher, more justifiable purpose. I also gave birth to a huge, ugly monster called debt. In time it would entice, seduce, and stalk me. I allowed it to do everything it could to destroy me, my marriage and my home. When it came to money, I did everything wrong.

Sure, we made pretty good money during those years. But I consistently and impulsively overspent our income. The more we made, the more I spent. More was never enough. When Harold's raises and promotions didn't come fast enough, I would demand that he find some way to refinance the house. Inevitably we would end up spending our precious equity to cover late fees and exorbitant interest charges in our never-ending quest to "catch up."

In time our ordinary living expenses plus the minimum monthly payments on the constantly growing debt monster exceeded our monthly income. Keeping food on the table and the house payment reasonably current became the emergencies that sent us in search of new sources of credit, higher credit limits, additional cash advances—loans from any source on any terms.

My turning point came one Saturday in 1982. I woke up from my marathon debting-spree to find my husband unemployed with no unemployment benefits, absolutely no income, and over $100,000 in unsecured debt. I was overcome with terror and panic. Like a cornered animal I felt as if there was no way out, no solution and everyone was out to get a piece of me. We were doomed to lose everything that mattered.

Never have I felt so lonely, so abandoned, and so helpless. For the first time in my life I was completely out of ideas. My schemes had failed along with all of my clever back-up plans. I was at the end of the line, I was tired and there was nothing I wanted to do more than give up. It is difficult to describe the unrelenting pain I carried in the pit of my stomach. So debilitating was my situation I couldn't even talk about it. To say that the communication between Harold and me was less than desirable is an understatement. At the time in our lives when we needed each other the most, we were the least able to reach out.

As I sunk to my all-time low there was nothing I could do but fall on my face completely broken and repentant before the One who knows me best and loves me most. I begged God to forgive me for the terrible mess I'd brought upon myself and my family. I confessed my penchant for lying, for deceiving in order to work things out on my own. I unconditionally promised that I would do whatever it took to turn this horrible situation around, to pay back the debt and change my ways. Since I was already in confessional mode I humbled myself even further by admitting to God that I had absolutely no idea where to start or what to do.

I wish I could say that at that very moment a brilliant light burst through the window as I was kneeling on the kitchen floor with my face buried in an overstuffed rocking chair. If only a loud voice had emanated from the brilliance announcing that all our debts were miraculously paid in full, our credit slate wiped clean. If only I could report that at that very moment I was supernaturally endowed with an invisible, impenetrable protective shield which would fortify me against ever again being tempted by the seductive lures of the credit industry. If that had happened, I would have a very happy publisher because this book would be guaranteed a permanent position at the top of the bestseller list.

Aren't we all secretly looking for miracles that will let us off the hook? Magic pills that will instantly fix everything? I received no such intervention, no magic. I suppose it is a good thing too, because had the solution been handed to me on such a scintillating platter I doubt I would have ever undergone the personal transformation that I have. Had my personal financial recovery been simple I might have been too easily persuaded to return to the foolishness that got me in trouble in the first place. Pain and fear are fantastic motivators, and was I ever motivated.

Change for me was a process which began ten days later. I received a phone call which would alter our lives. I agreed to accept a two-fold employment position. I became both a property manager for several large industrial developments and a real estate agent selling and leasing industrial properties. Hard work? Yes. Stressful work? At times. Wonderful opportunity? The best. With my new job came a big change on the home front. As I became the breadwinner, Harold became the home keeper. Switching roles turned out to be an excellent move. Jeremy and Josh got to spend a lot of time with their Dad, and I had an opportunity to test my resolve to do whatever was necessary to pay back the debt and change my ways. I learned firsthand how difficult it can be to earn a living.

I came to the point that I acknowledged the true source of my income. I determined that I'd spent my last moment worrying about from where the money would come. I realized for the first time in my life that my employer (or my parents, investment portfolio, pensions, bonuses, rental income, unemployment checks, gifts from family and friends or any other entity) was not the source of my income. These were simply channels through which I received money. The source is God who'd given me abilities and skills. I determined that never again would I fear the loss of my job, the fall of real estate values, the stock market or any other economic disaster. I could relax confident in the fact that the channels through which I receive money may come and go, but my source is the same yesterday, today and tomorrow. Never again would I mistake the channel for the source nor would I shirk my responsibility to perform to the very best of my ability.

Our spending habits immediately changed dramatically. Over the following months and years we learned to cut and cut. And cut. And cut some more. I can't say we did everything right. Because we didn't share our situation with anyone and sought no outside help we missed out on an important aspect which would have surely sped up our resolve to live debt-free.

There is something cathartic about telling another person about your situation and plan to change that situation. In 1992 I had one major cathartic experience.

By that time we had struggled through 10 years of financial recovery. We'd done the old three-steps-forward two-steps-back routine. We didn't have a good master plan and treated the entire situation as a deep dark and embarrassing secret known only to the two of us. We stumbled more than once which did nothing more than delay the time it would take to reach our goal of becoming debt-free. By this time we had paid back the major portion of the debt; we had started our own real estate company and things were going well. But the debt repayment was taking much too long. I was becoming impatient and began looking for a way I could bring fresh new excitement into my life and at the same time make enough additional income to get rid of the debt once and for all.

My search ended when I got the wild idea to write and publish a subscription newsletter. I had the equipment in place, I had a modicum of computer knowledge, and I sure knew the subject matter. After a few months of planning and strategizing *Cheapskate Monthly* was born on January 1, 1992.

In the first issue I gave a very abbreviated version of my story, the mess I'd made, and the journey we were taking toward recovery. I had learned to affectionately refer to myself as a "cheapskate" because that was the best word I could come up with which defined the radical changes I had learned to make. I redefined a cheapskate to be one who saves consistently, gives generously, and never spends more than he or she has.

Within a very short time I felt as if someone had turned on a faucet. Subscriptions started pouring in, the media started calling and I had to get a bigger post office box. Hundreds of letters began pouring in. Time and time again I would open a letter which would begin, "Dear Mary: I've never told anyone what I'm about to tell you . . ." and then the floodgates would open. With each successive issue of CM I would open my heart further which in turn would encourage readers to do the same. As I became accountable to thousands of people throughout the U.S. and Canada my own personal recovery began to speed up.

As I began reading everything I could get my hands on in preparation for writing a new issue each month I began to understand where I'd been, why I did what I'd done and how far I'd come. I found validation in learning that much of we had done in order to get back on the right financial track was exactly right, and I had moments of regret and sadness as I admitted that we'd blown it on more than one occasion.

One of the most remarkable things I learned was that which I'd considered my unique problem was shared by many others. I even discovered people in situations worse than mine. But the wonderful thing was the sense of fellowship. In time I would receive so many letters that answering them became my number one challenge, but I couldn't ignore them because these were people who needed me as much as I needed them. As I would write reply after reply I could feel myself becoming stronger. The more I shared of my own recovery struggle, the more easily I was able to reject the constant opportunities to return to my old ways.

In time I began speaking publicly, telling my story and offering hope and encouragement to others. Soon I found myself living my recovery in fast-forward mode and in the public spotlight.

Some time during that first year I was offered a book contract which I accepted and miraculously found time to write. Once the book was published the faucet turned on full-blast and the letters started coming faster and faster. I received letters of desperation, fear, panic, success, joy and thankfulness. You name the emotion or situation and I believe I have at least one letter in my files that fits it to a tee.

So did we reach our goal? Yes. Do we have new goals? Yes. Have I recovered? No. I will always be in-process with my recovery. It is a step-by-step proposition for me. I still struggle with the temptations of overspending, getting into debt and having today what I'd rather pay for next year. I handle it much better now than I did before. I can go for days without being tempted. And I find that speaking out and helping others, encouraging those who are in the financial pits, encourages me. It's a lot like physical fitness. The more I work at my recovery, the stronger I get. But I need to work out regularly or I am sure to weaken and become susceptible to a major backslide.

. . . today has been the most stressful of all days of my financial worries.

"I am a 34-year-old homemaker. I have two children and left a lucrative career to stay home with them thinking I could and would make the necessary sacrifices. However, once my unemployment ran out I slowly started to get into debt. We just weren't making it on my husband's income alone.

When I quit work I had approximately $4,000 in credit card debt and a personal loan of $5,000. While I worked I lived from payday to payday and after ten years I really didn't have anything to show for it except maybe a closet full of clothes. I was always responsible for my own debts and my husband his.

When I quit I received a $20,000 severance which was to have gone to my mother to repay the $15,000 she lent us to purchase our home. But instead I paid off the personal loan ($5,000) and spent the rest on I don't know what.

I then started borrowing funds a little at a time from my mother's account to cover my overdrafts (I had signing authority but up until now she had no idea.) I just thought, "Oh, I'll be able to start paying it back every payday," but that never seemed to happen. Now she knows and is furious with me. I owe her about $25,000.

This, combined with my husband being totally unaware of our obligations, has caused me immense stress. He has no idea that I've used his credit cards for cash advances to the tune of $7,000 and that I've remortgaged our home twice now without his knowledge.

My total debt is approximately $130,000 and my husband thinks it is $60,000. I can't talk to him—he would never understand.

Sometimes I think the only way out is the coward's way. If I were to pass on our home would be paid for, my personal loan would be paid for (insurance) and my husband and children would get a $150,000 life insurance policy.

I feel like I am going to lose it all—my sanity, my family, everything. Right now I feel so ashamed and embarrassed. I hardly ever leave the house . . .

Rita

CHAPTER 2

What I've Learned

I never dreamed that anyone would ever consider me an expert on money management. Why should they? I am probably by nature the all-time worst manager of money who ever planted two feet on this earth. I am thankful, however, that I am not destined to remain in my natural state. I've learned that I can change my attitude, my behavior and my insatiable desires. I've learned how to control my spending and I've learned the joy of living debt-free. I'm basking in the freedom and happiness of living *beneath* our income, meager as it may be at times.

So am I an expert? Before you decide please remember what I am not. I am not a certified financial planner, an accountant, or attorney. I am not an economist, stockbroker, or master of business administration. I am not a psychologist or marriage counselor. I am not able to perform miracles.

What I am is a recovered credit card junkie who's

taken back control of her life. I am practical minded, realistic and totally convinced that a sense of humor is the best way to deal with life's curve balls. I am skilled at dealing with creditors and bill collectors. I only offer advice which is based on proven experience. I strive to be nonjudgmental and trustworthy, understanding and caring. But most of all, I am anxious to help you find practical solutions to your own financial situation.

So if this qualifies me as some kind of an expert, well . . . I can deal with that!

My life has changed radically during the past three years since I came out of the closet, so to speak. I broke my self-imposed gag order and told the whole world about my struggle with a debilitating spending addiction. I had no idea at the time that this would be one of the smartest things I could ever do. You see, by telling my story and owning up to my problem I became accountable.

In the past three years I've read and written hundreds of thousands of words on the subject of money management. I've experimented with this method and that. My mail has become so voluminous that a turbo-charged power letter opener has become my personal favorite in office accessories. I've read thousands of pages of personal and confidential stories. Some are hilarious, others moving, some even tragic. I've analyzed untold individual situations. I've addressed audiences large and small. I've listened, pondered, and asked questions. I've collected enough data to choke a well-adjusted accountant.

As I have absorbed all of this information, stirred it up, and boiled it down I am amazed to see how many common threads run through situation after situation.

Have I come up with any conclusions? Thousands, to be exact, but my most important conclusion is: Anyone can learn to control their spending.

If you are experiencing financial trouble it can undoubtedly be traced back to the time that you first failed to control your spending. And the trouble just started to grow. And for some of us it grew and grew. And others of us? It grew and grew and grew and grew. And grew some more.

I'm not so sure we can trust statistics, however, I tend to believe the ones that support my theories. That's why I always quote the statistic that says only 10 percent of the U.S. population knows how to control their spending. I've lived, breathed, eaten, smelled, and tasted money management and financial fixing around the clock now for 12 years and I have come up with a few more conclusions:

1. Most people who think they are in hopelessly dire financial straits aren't as badly off as they fear.
2. With determination and commitment most situations can be turned around quickly.
3. Even the worst situations are not completely hopeless.

My fascination with personal financial situations sent me on a crusade to find out why so many people get into money trouble. Not only is this a problem of epidemic proportions, talking about it is probably the only taboo left in our tell-all society. I've concluded that regardless of our attitudes about money, the amount of money we have, or any other individual factors, these are the main reasons so many people are experiencing money problems:

1. Money problems are rooted in one's refusal to accept the fact that life is not fair.

A terrible disorder is running rampant in this country. I call it *entitle-itis*. We feel entitled to all kinds of material things equal or better than what everyone else has. In essence we demand that life be fair, that we are entitled to all kinds of stuff just like our friends and neighbors. We have swallowed hook, line, and sinker the notion that we have a right to all the gusto because we only go around once and we have to get it all now! And when our incomes don't quite cut it we feel entitled to credit sufficient to keep the score even.

2. Money problems are the result of irregular, intermittent or unpredictable expenses.

Very few people have clear knowledge of their true expenses. Because they are do not consider intermittent and irregular expenses as regular monthly obligations, these expenses turn into emergencies and financial crises.

3. Money problems will never go away as long as debt is carried over from month to month.

Unsecured debt and its merciless interest has an odd way of reproducing itself. It never stays the same and if it doesn't shrink it grows.

I've learned how to turn things around, how to get out of debt and stay out of debt, how to start a real savings program, how to become a giver, and how to live honestly and joyfully. I know how it feels to get off the roller coaster and stay on level ground where money ceases to be an issue. I've learned that financial ease has nothing to do with being rich.

I also know that whether your financial situation requires a minor correction or a major overhaul, no situation is hopeless. You can take back control of your finances.

Regaining control over your situation is not only possible—provided you follow through first by finishing this book—it is highly probable. By following the logical, well-principled, and simple steps I am going to teach you, you can expect to be back in the driver's seat of your money life very soon.

Not that this is going to be a quick-fix, Band-Aid approach to your current situation. This Money Makeover is not some new and unique way to teach you how to organize your spending so that you can more easily live with your debt or rearrange your financial statement to help you qualify for new debt. That won't work. We're going to tackle the root problems, and then I'm going to teach you some simple and very effective ways to regain control of your finances and your life.

CHAPTER 3

Are You a Good Money Makeover Candidate?

Makeovers. Wonderful, aren't they? Someone waves a magic wand and poof—everything that was ugly is magically new and remarkably gorgeous.

My favorite makeovers are the ones featured on television shows because I don't have to wait for the results. Through the miracle of TV I get to see the pathetic "before" at the beginning of the show and the sensational "after" at the end. I do exactly what the show producers hope I will: I watch the entire show just to see the makeover result.

Call me overly sentimental, but I actually cried when the unsuspecting lady of the house opened the door of her home that had been given a complete decorating makeover compliments of daytime TV's most popular talk show. She cried and so I cried, too. Mostly out of jealousy, I'm sure. They spent big bucks to make sure this was a successful show and it worked.

Makeover. It's an amazing word that says, "You aren't looking that great. You could use some improvement. You need help. I can fix you."

Makes you wonder how those people in the magazines and on the TV shows feel when they receive the phone call offering them a makeover. Or how about the homes, faces or bodies they consider and then pass over?! How would you like to be considered for a makeover and then rejected for lack of potential? That could require some serious couch time.

But not every face nor every home needs a makeover. Imagine the lunacy of a popular magazine offering to do a makeover on Cindy Crawford or a home improvement show calling the White House to offer their services.

So where do you stand in the Money Makeover department? Are you a hopeless case or are you in such good shape a Money Makeover would not only be useless, that even to consider such silliness would be an insult to your fine money management skills?

The fact that you picked up this book leads me to believe that there is a possibility a tiny bit of improvement might be welcomed, but do you qualify for a makeover?

Basically there are only two requirements to qualify for a Money Makeover. Desire and capacity. If you are ready to take back control of your finances, relieve the stress which money has created, and prepare for the future then you are more than qualified in the desire category. If you earn money and are obligated to pay bills you also have the capacity.

Whether or not you need a Money Makeover is up to you. If you are experiencing joy and an absence of stress, the few bills that you do have are paid on time, you are not rolling over debt from one month to the next, you feel well-prepared for the future and unexpected financial obligations do not side-track or concern you, congratulations! You really don't need a Money Makeover. In fact, you should get in that other line with Cindy Crawford.

Now for the rest of us (yes, I put myself in the makeover-in-progress category because my own makeover maintenance is a day-by-day endeavor) I can't think of too many situations which would not profit from the benefits of a Money Makeover. Perhaps you only need a minor adjustment to get your-self into the fast lane of financial ease. Or maybe you have been derailed for some time and require more intensive work to get yourself back on track and rolling again.

Let me assure you that most people will benefit from this Money Makeover. In fact, I get excited just thinking about starting you on the makeover. The process is simple and based upon solid financial principles. You will not learn how to cheat your creditors or lie to credit reporting agencies. You will not be encouraged to do anything illegal, unethical, immoral, or stupid.

If you have the ability to mess up your financial life, then you certainly have the ability to turn it around. You will be required to work. No magic wands here. You might have to break some destructive habits. You will have to learn how to be honest. If self-discipline has been missing on your list of personal characteristics that will have to change, but the change will be relatively painless because of the tremendous joy you will begin to experience immediately.

Following are some real and recurring financial situations. See if any of these scenarios sound at all familiar.

Situation #1: You get an income tax refund because you generously overpaid the government last year, asking them to keep what they need and send you the balance sometime after April 15—without interest, of course. Since you can't decide whether to put the money towards an outstanding debt or replace your antique, beyond-repair washing machine, you "wisely" put the money into your checking account so you won't be tempted to spend it. A month or so later you decide the washing machine replacement idea has moved from optional to obligatory. You check your current checking account balance and are flabbergasted when you realize that the money is gone! (This also causes a few cross words with your spouse because this kind of thing is always the other person's fault). Somehow the entire tax refund has been absorbed into your everyday living expenses. Since you have to get a washing machine and you no longer have cash which

would've allowed you to consider a good used machine, you reluctantly go ahead and purchase a new
one on credit.

Situation #2: Things have been going pretty well
for a while and for the first time in a long time you
actually have a few bucks left at the end of the
month. You decide to go ahead and get the new
patio furniture you've been eyeing. No sooner is the
beautiful set delivered, than without any warning,
your car breaks down. There's no way you could
have predicted this. And the prognosis is not good.
You need major repairs which are going to cost over
$600. Just what you need! Another crisis. Since you
have no excess cash in the old checking account and
no savings, you have no choice but to go to the bank
and take a cash advance on your credit card. This
emergency is so dire you don't even worry about the
interest rate. You are just happy that at least the
credit is available.

Situation #3: You've been planning a family vacation. The kids are excited and you really need to get
away. You've been meaning to start saving for the
trip, but something seems to come up every month
and well, you just haven't been able to get started.
Before you know it, it's time to make the reservations and you don't have dime-one to pay for them.
You rationalize that family time is a priority, that this
trip is a once-in-a-lifetime opportunity and what the
heck, you work hard and you deserve a vacation just

like all of your friends and coworkers. You promise yourself you will put the trip on your credit cards but will make huge payments when you get home to pay it off quickly. (How many times have you said that before?)

Leaving town with credit cards in tow gives you a feeling of security and entitlement. Now is certainly not the time to worry about the cost of things. You want to show the family a good time.

Situation #4: You've lived in the house for seven years (could it possibly be that long?!) and you still don't have living room furniture. The master bedroom looks the same as it did the day you moved in and will look gorgeous as soon as you get a little extra cash to decorate. You have plans—you know exactly how you want to decorate and furnish those rooms—as soon as you get some extra money. Weeks, months and years keep flying by and still no extra money. You are embarrassed about how the place looks so you find yourself avoiding guests. Every time you visit others' homes you feel pitiful and envious and leave feeling unhappy about your own home.

Situation #5: You carry $250 deductible on your auto insurance in order to get the lower semiannual premiums. Wouldn't you know it? The one and only time you forget to look behind you before pulling out of the grocery store parking lot you smack a stupid little pole so hard you ram the rear fender right into the rear wheel. Total repairs? $1,200! You just don't have an extra $250 for the deductible, but your car is not drivable. What choice do you have? Your credit cards are all maxed out. Financial disasters don't often give a warning so how in the world were you supposed to plan ahead? You are forced to go to your parents. They reluctantly spring for the cash, but you know what's going to happen. You are surely in for another lecture and until you pay them back you are going to feel guilty. The last time you borrowed from them you were miserable. They made you feel like a little kid again. It was like they owned you. If you were even a day late with the payment you got that look and the cold shoulder. When you owe them money your relationship is affected negatively. You just hate doing this, but what alternatives do you have? You can't live without a car.

Situation #6: You just moved into a new apartment, one with lots of windows and daylight. You are thoroughly ashamed of your living room furniture which you realized was a bit tired in the old place but has suddenly dropped to horrible in its new surroundings. You just happen to read a flyer in the newspaper announcing a going-out-of-business furniture sale. You drop in just to see what they have and drop out an hour later with a nifty easy-payment contract in your pocket. You are tickled with how easily you were able to arrange financing on an eight-piece collection with classic French styling in the tradition of Master European Craftsmen. Who cares what the financing charges are? You were able to pull this off with no money down!

Situation #7: You have a secret that is eating you alive. You have run up nearly $12,000 in credit card debt during the last year alone and your wife has absolutely no idea. You handle the family finances and while it's been tough you've been able to juggle pretty well to keep her from finding out. When you took a slight pay cut last year getting a few new pre-approved credit cards seemed like a prudent thing to do—just in case of emergency. You didn't mention them to her because you knew it would just make her worry more about the money situation, and she depends so much on your ability to handle money. You didn't intend to start using the cards, but they seemed so available and with the household funds being so tight temporarily (the company promised to restore your pay rate as soon as possible) paying for things with the cards did seem like the best way.

A year later your salary has not increased, but your debt sure has. You've arranged to have the bills sent to the office, and creditors are starting to call you at work because you just can't keep up with those payments. You're scared to death that your wife or boss will find out. You see no way out but to apply for more loans just to keep the minimum monthly payments current.

* * *

If you identified with any of these real life situations, you will definitely benefit from a Money Makeover. I want to show you how to handle your money so that these situations (which happen to everyone) won't disrupt your life. I want to teach you how to prepare for them, how to rework your finances so that you can relax and enjoy life. I'm even going to convince you to get out of debt. And I'm going to show you how to do it quickly—not the so-slow-that-I-will-pay-lots-of-interest way that your creditors have in mind.

Still not convinced that a Money Makeover should be in your future? Grab a pencil and take the following mini-quiz. Simply answer "yes" or "no."

1. I spend most of my take-home income on paying credit card bills.

2. I am near, at, or over the limit on my lines of credit.

3. I am habitually late paying my bills.

4. I often pay late penalties.

5. I make only the minimum payment on my charge accounts.

6. I have to pay half my bills one month and half the next month because I can't pay all of them at the same time.

7. I write postdated checks.

8. I've bounced three checks in the last year.

9. I often "overshop" to meet the minimum-purchase requirement for credit card transactions.

10. I've taken a cash advance on one credit card to make the payment on another card.

11. I have to work overtime just to meet my current financial obligations.

12. I am unable to estimate how much I owe in installment debts.

13. I worry about money quite a bit.

14. I do not have a regular savings program.

15. I carry a balance from month to month on at least one credit card and keep hoping to pay it off completely, someday.

16. Some months I do pretty well, and then other months I'm really caught off guard by unexpected expenses.

17. I live from paycheck to paycheck and would be in big trouble if I lost my job.

18. I'd love to be able to make charitable contributions, but forget it. There's just not enough money to go around. I am my own favorite charity.

19. If I made more money I'd be just fine.

20. I'm in really big trouble. Creditors are calling all the time and I just don't know how long I'll be able to juggle everything. I'm really scared.

21. I feel mature and grown up when I use credit cards.

22. I use credit cards to buy things I would never purchase with cash.

23. I spend money because I expect my income to increase.

24. I have applied for more than five credit cards in the past year.

25. I regularly pay for groceries with a credit card because I have to.

26. My credit cards make me feel rich.

27. I like to collect cash from friends in restaurants, then charge the bill to my credit card.

28. I can't imagine living without credit.

29. I have lied to my spouse or creditors about making payments.

30. I worry everytime the phone rings.

If you answered "no" to all of the foregoing you obviously know how to control your spending and are enjoying the sense of personal accomplishment which comes from managing your resources in an intelligent and reasonable manner.

If you answered "yes" to no more than three questions you are probably okay for now, but should consider this a warning sign. Unless you change your ways problems do lie ahead for you. A Money Makeover is probably the very best thing you could do to stop heading downhill.

If you answered "yes" to four or more questions, you definitely need me.

So that you don't think you are alone, let me share some of the information I have gleaned from researching the subject and corresponding with the thousands of people who have written to me in the past three years.

Ninety percent of your friends and relatives know very little about money management. Eighty percent of all Americans have never had a savings account and only 10 percent of the total population have any idea how to control their spending.

There are approximately *1 billion* active credit cards in this country as of this writing. Statistics say only 28 percent of those cardholders pay their balances in full every 30 days. That means *720 million* credit card accounts carry balances month after month, year after year. This represents millions of people who are hopelessly doomed to live their lives imprisoned by perma-debt. (Perma-debt is that dreadful condition brought about by revolving debt which rolls over from month to month, year to year, decade to decade and follows its victim right to the grave.)

So why do so few people actually do something about their financial woes? Partly because a major characteristic of human nature is laziness. A lot of people are looking for a no-effort way to make their lives perfect. They want someone to fix their problems. Believe it or not, I've found that a great majority of those people in the greatest financial trouble are willing to remain miserable until they win the lottery or are surprised by some big inheritance. While waiting they continue to live in misery, limping through life, complaining all the way.

Many Americans have gotten into a very bad habit of demanding "it" now and paying for "it" later. We have learned to feel entitled and think nothing of accepting 36 easy payments and a myriad of other marketing ploys. Hopefully before too many more pages you will be convinced that living this way is not going to do anything but keep you headed in a downward spiral, a killer spiral of uncontrollable debt and misery.

I believe there are many people who sincerely want to do something about their out-of-control financial situations, but don't know how. Where do they go to find help—practical, affordable, and effective help? For those in major crises there are 12-Step programs, credit counseling organizations, and bankruptcy protection. But most people have not reached the point of requiring such intensive and dramatic intervention. A reasonable alternative is the Money Makeover.

If you are lazy and have no intention of working at your own makeover, you will not be successful because I promise you no miracles, no magic. What I can promise is that if you carefully follow this plan you will experience remarkable results. You are going to be very pleased with your "after" picture!

CHAPTER 4

This is Not a Budget

I hate the word *budget*. You're probably relieved to hear that because you've undoubtedly grown to dread the whole idea of a budget. More than likely the reason we detest the b-word is that it reminds us of a diet and both diets and budgets translate to a straitjacket, mean and confining.

Frankly, I don't think budgets work. I don't believe that living under the domination of some standardized formula that ties you up and keeps you in a constant state of confinement produces true economic freedom or financial ease. If you are fearful that this Money Makeover is going to require you fit into some slick newfangled budget I've designed, you can breathe a sigh of relief.

Like diets, I suppose any kind of budget "works" for a short while. (No matter what diet you go on, you will lose weight, too.) But anything that is rigid, confining and depriving will eventually be abandoned whether it's a diet or a budget. The weight invariably comes back, as do the bad money management practices, and usually in much larger proportions, too.

If you have tried going on a budget you know the feeling of failure and hopelessness when you finally fell off the wagon, back to your old ways of unbridled spending, attempting to keep just one step ahead of your creditors.

A budget doesn't work because it controls your life. Most people don't like to be told what to do. Undoubtedly that has something to do with why prisoners aren't the happiest people in the world and teenagers can't wait to get out on their own. It is human nature to want to be in control of one's life.

A budget doesn't work because it is typically a rigid set of rules taken from the pages of some financial text or other impersonal source full of theories and national averages. A budget feels like a punishment. I'm not saying that rules are always bad but when it comes to a family's finances, my experience has been that rigid rules imposed by outside sources don't seem to work. I'm only being practical and realistic. Rules make you feel bad. They have a way of inducing guilt even when guilt is not warranted. They typically leave no leeway for adjustment.

I also don't like budgets because they ignore the root problem. Without taking care of what's going on on the inside, simply wriggling into a stiff ill-fitting budget will do nothing but mask the symptoms without treating the attitudes which led to the problem in the first place.

Budgets don't work because the word budget has a negative connotation. Budget stands for scarcity, deprivation and an absence of spontaneity and joy. Usually the word budget emanates from the mouth of a strict parent, an out-of-touch financial planner, or a wealthy tax advisor. Most people who try to budget are defeated before they begin because of their preconceived prejudices.

So if budgets don't work, is there an alternative that does? If diets don't work to produce permanent weight loss, is there anything that does? Yes! A complete lifestyle change. Anyone who has successfully lost weight and kept it off will tell you that they permanently changed their eating habits in a way that fit their individual lifestyle. They will surely report that they have learned to incorporate physical activity into their life and that they finally made the change for themselves instead of to please others or comply with some weight chart or commercial dictatorial regimen. Nor did they deprive themselves temporarily, secretly planning that when the weight finally came off they would be able to return to their favorite foods and sedentary lifestyle.

So are you convinced that this is not another budget book? I truly hope so.

The successful alternative to a budget is a plan, a blueprint for your financial future.

I love the concept of a plan. With plans cities are built, battles are won, and chaos is turned to order.

You need a financial plan for today, tomorrow, a month from now, a year from now, right on through your retirement. You must design a plan that works for you. It has to be tailor-made for your lifestyle, your needs, your goals. With a plan, *you* control your finances, *you* slip into the driver's seat of your money life. With a spending plan you can really become the manager of your future instead of just letting life happen to you.

Of course it is all going to look great on paper, but execution and implementation are quite another matter. It's going to be mandatory that you follow through on your planning. This will require discipline. But let me assure you, the success you will experience from the outset is going to be the catalyst to keep you executing and implementing. You're going to love what follows. I promise.

If you and I have anything at all in common, it may be this: We flinch at the thought of anyone telling us what to do. Or spend. Or eat. Or anything! "It's a free country, I'm an adult and I'll do whatever I please, thank-you. I'll do it my way, when I'm good and ready so just get off my back and don't bug me."

As a teenager I couldn't wait to leave home. I wanted to get out there where no one could tell me what to do. I didn't want to have to explain why I did what I did with whom or how much it cost. In my mind the less accountability the greater the freedom. That attitude affected my life from my bank account, to my automobile maintenance, to my eating habits.

Ironically I lived for approval and was constantly aware of what people might think. My days were dominated with figuring out what I could do to get people to approve of me. I tried to be good, bought beautiful gifts, gave musical performances, and tried to present an acceptable appearance.

I needed the approval of everyone around me from the cashier at the department store (I didn't want her to think I was cheap or couldn't afford anything I wanted) to the grocery store clerk, to friends and relatives. I had to do things well, I had to entertain well, I had to be the best, but only to gain outside approval. I didn't require any kind of approval from within. I would sell myself and my future down the river just to earn the momentary approval of others. My approval rating system demanded I go into major debt every Christmas to buy things that without doubt would be forgotten by New Year's Day.

It cost me dearly to learn this very valuable lesson: Accountability is the key to freedom. This is a principle you must accept on faith. It is true believe me. The absence of accountability in my life led to unbearable financial bondage. I became hopelessly buried by a mountain of killer debt. I couldn't be bothered with saving for the future. If it felt good, I did it, and spending money felt darned good. I became addicted to always spending more than we made. I had no idea where all the money went and it was a rare occasion indeed that I would even record the checks I wrote. But no one told *me* what to do! No sirree. No one, that is, except the bill collectors, the IRS, the mortgage holder, the county tax collector and the utility companies.

It still sounds crazy to me, but I know that it is true: The more accountable I become, the greater my freedom. The more I am willing to become disciplined the more numerous my options. The more carefully I plan, and the bigger I dream, the better my life becomes and the more joy I experience. I am probably the most naturally undisciplined person on the face of the earth, but I have discovered and developed within myself the discipline and the strength to change. I am no one unusual or extraordinary. I just did a complete "one-eighty" on the road to self-destruction. My makeover has been so dramatic that sometimes I don't even recognize myself, and that, I have to tell you, is a terrific feeling.

It doesn't matter if you feel you are beyond hope, or if you have just set foot down that self-destruction road, you can change. You can turn around and get going in the right direction. I'm glad you've asked me to show you how.

This is not a budget. It is a new way of life.

CHAPTER 5

Money Beliefs

What is money? Ask a four-year-old. You will learn that money is round, dimes are smaller than nickels, pennies are brown, and quarters are big.

Ask the same question of someone with more life experience and you will get a variety of one-word answers: power, freedom, security, pleasure, choices.

Based upon the tons of mail I receive and my own experiences, I have concluded that most of us merely dream about money. We fantasize about this elusive power, freedom, happiness, pleasure, and security which we are convinced will naturally result— just as soon as we figure out how to get enough money. We do this because we have a distorted and unrealistic view of money and what it can do. When it comes to money, many of us live under false beliefs which greatly affect our lives.

The roles money plays

Basically all money beliefs are a version of two basic alternate beliefs: Money is good; money is evil. Whether we worship money or hate it, when we hold it responsible for our happiness we give it power. Whether consciously or subconsciously, we choose the role money plays in our lives. We, not our money, are solely responsible for our attitudes, beliefs, actions, and our happiness.

What role does money play in your life? Is it your best friend or your worst enemy?

Since you've probably not spent much time thinking about what role money plays in your life, the following are some ideas to get you started. Study them carefully. Perhaps none will describe your feelings exactly, but I can promise these ideas will start you thinking in a new way which, in turn, will help you discover what kind of a relationship you have with money.

Money as a tranquilizer

Money can be one of life's most powerful mood changers. Spending it can be as mood-altering as drugs or alcohol, and as habit-forming. If you are carrying around huge credit card balances I would venture to say that you frequently spend compulsively in an attempt to change your mood.

It is very easy to get caught up in this habit of

looking to money to change our moods. It is socially acceptable and nonfattening. It's not hard to convince ourselves we deserve something new because we feel a little blue, are lonely, need love, are bored, or have really suffered through a rotten week.

When it comes to chasing away a black cloud there's no denying that spending money certainly does the trick. A trip to the mall with credit cards in tow used to be my antidepressant of choice. Spending helped me forget my troubles and it just felt good to buy something. I frequently promised myself that this was the last time, that I would start a new budget tomorrow. Buying something *on sale* always made me feel righteous which added to the legitimacy of the act. Because I was convinced that spending money would change my mood, it always did.

Worshiping money

If I asked you point blank, "Do you worship money?" you would offer a resounding, "No!"

Not surprising.

We are conditioned to find the very idea of worshiping money to be highly offensive, and as such, dismiss the thought as ludicrous.

Worship is a conscious action which must involve three things: an object to be worshiped, a worshiper and the voluntary submission of the worshiper to the object of worship. The worshiper expresses love, fear, awe, and gratitude to and for the object and voluntarily gives up control to the thing or person worshiped.

I grew up in a very religious environment. As a youngster I learned a lot—most of which I didn't understand. There was one thing, however, that I did understand but wished I didn't. That was the part about the love of money being the root of all evil. That axiom always bothered me terribly because, well . . . I loved money! Pure and simple. And I wasn't really wild about that evil part. I worried about how I would know if I started loving money too much. It bothered me so much that I finally dismissed the whole problem in my usual fashion—I decided to not think about it. I learned at a very young age the benefits of slipping into denial when reality became unbearable.

It was a gradual thing, but by the time I reached adulthood I had given money full authority to ascend to the throne of my life. I turned over control of my life to it, I loved it, and stood in awe of what I believed it could do. If I'd been confronted about my relationship with money I would have denied that I worshiped it. Of course, I would *say* that money cannot buy happiness, but I didn't really believe it. Quite the contrary, I was secretly convinced that money, enough of it, held all the keys to making my life perfect.

I manipulated what I knew to be true because I couldn't conceive of anything quite so horrible as worshiping money. I had to find ways to mask the truth which is how I got so good at living in denial. There is no doubt in my mind that my love of money was the root of all kinds of evil in my life. It has taken a long time to peel back all of the denial and distorted thinking, acknowledge the painful truth, deal with it appropriately, and find the proper role for money in my life.

I don't intend to get into a long theological study, mostly because I am not qualified to do so. However, I sincerely believe that every person is born with a God-shaped hole in his or her heart, which from the moment of birth demands to be filled. But we're clever humans and we try to cram all kinds of things into that empty place, things that don't fit— things like money or people or possessions, for instance. Nothing or no one but the God of the universe himself can fill that place in our lives. He fits perfectly. When we get things in the right order we learn to worship God and use money. Then our lives take on meaning and order.

For the person who worships money, getting more and more of it becomes the central focus and driving force of every life action. Because the ego is insatiable, more money is never enough and because the majority of us are not wealthy and never will be, if we worship money we've guaranteed ourselves a life of unhappiness. We're always waiting to be happy until we have enough money—which will be never.

Money proves success

Many of us have grown up with the belief that success and wealth automatically travel hand-in-hand. We have even come to believe that wealthy people are happier than we are because of their riches, and they're better than we are because wealth is a reward for goodness. We relate poverty with evil and prosperity with good. We subconsciously feel that poor people are a few bricks shy of a load in the intelligence department, to say nothing of the fact they are downright lazy!

Those of us who believe that wealth equals success run into real trouble if we ever, God forbid, find ourselves lacking in the money department. We have to deny, cover up, lie about, and hide the problem because having no money would surely mean we are lazy, unsuccessful, and deserving of very little, if any, approval. We don't like to feel badly about ourselves. When we lack money we feel like failures; if we have good luck with money, then we feel successful.

Credit cards were invented with wealth-equals-success folks in mind. When required to live on our meager incomes we feel poor and unsuccessful, but as we are able to get our hands on significant quantities of "plastic money" we instantly feel successful and just a little bit better than those with less.

Maybe we learned this particular belief from childhood fairy tales. The good boys and girls marry princesses and princes, reside in castles and live happily ever after. The bad are driven to the streets to beg and live in misery. Good people are rich. Bad people are poor. And depending upon the fluctuations our current bank balance we can go all the way from being good to being bad within a matter of days. To say we ride an emotional roller coaster is an understatement.

Money proves self-worth

Many of us believe the myth that money somehow determines our personal worth. We base our self-concept on how much money we have or don't have. Those of us who operate under the belief that money equals worth set ourselves up for potential trouble.

Consider the young businessman who owns and operates a lucrative business. During the good times if his financial worth determines his personal worth, he sits on top of the world exuding self-confidence, strength and leadership. But what happens to his self-esteem when the company hits the skids during the lean, recessionary times? If he loses his shirt in business his self-concept goes right down the drain along with it.

While this is quite similar to the money-equals-success role, it does carry one distinct difference. Because one's personal worth is a self-esteem issue it is not so easily changed. Once we are convinced we are worthless and that's why we are unable to attract money into our lives it is highly unlikely we will find the motivation necessary to do anything about what we consider a permanent condition. We feel destined to remain worthless and stumble through life feeling sorry for ourselves.

The belief that money proves self-worth can go two ways: "I must have a lot of money in order to prove I have worth," and "I have no worth, so I deserve little or no money."

I've been corresponding with Lucy for about a year now. Right from the start I noticed that she never asked anything of me, but rather was a constant source of encouragement and wisdom, always offering her support and counsel based upon the latest research on compulsive spending or whatever topic I happened to hit on in a recent issue of *Cheapskate Monthly*. Without fail she was able to say just the right thing to help me better understand myself and my struggles with compulsive behaviors. Her obvious love of books and ability to ferret out the best, offering insightful overviews and synopses of them, led me to believe that she was either a university professor, book reviewer, or professional in the field of literature or psychology. I was, and continue to be, very grateful for this smart lady who has become my valuable through-the-mail book reviewer.

Recently in one of my letters I inquired about her education and occupation. Perhaps you can understand my surprise when I read the following postscript from her latest letter:

P.S. I do not have a job in the literary world although I am a college graduate with highly developed verbal and reading skills who majored in English literature. I work a menial, one-dimensional job that almost any high school graduate could do. It's not a complex prestigious job that only a college graduate could handle. I am an office clerk for the federal government.

She went on to describe how she struggles financially, barely existing on an annual wage which hovers at the poverty level.

When we struggle with a very low opinion of ourselves and feel that we deserve only an amount of money which reflects that opinion, we sabotage our opportunities for making more money. We approach our finances with such fear and worry that we refuse to see ourselves as worthy of anything better. We get exactly what we feel we deserve: a poverty-level income which keeps us forever stuck in a pitiful situation.

I believe that Lucy's situation may be the consequence of her belief that money proves worth. She feels destined to stay in a minimum wage position because that's exactly what she feels she's worth. She has chained herself to a job which is not fulfilling and does not provide her the joy and contentment she would find in a career which challenges her natural talents and abilities. There's no doubt that Lucy has the ability to do great things and break away from the false beliefs which are holding her down and preventing her from experiencing a more abundant life and a sense of self-worth.

Money is evil

There are those of us who believe that money is basically evil, that those who have it are unscrupulous, sinister, insensitive, dishonest, corrupt, and just plain greedy.

If we believe this, then, of course, we are going to keep ourselves as happy as possible by espousing the evils of money. The poorer we can remain the cleaner, purer, and more virtuous (perhaps even more spiritual?) we will become. To welcome money into our lives would be to blatantly invite evil. Hate and fear of money become our unspoken rationale for losing, mishandling or being unable to handle money or even refusing to accept it. When we feel that money is evil we build a secret resentment and anger toward those who have more than we do which further justifies us labeling them as evil.

People who unconsciously hate money often end up feeling guilty if for some reason they have plenty of it, because after all they believe money to be the source of all evil. One common result is that they deny themselves and their family things which they could easily afford because of their rigid attitudes regarding needs versus wants. Their deep belief that the enjoyment of money is evil remains the driving force behind their Spartan existence. They hoard huge sums of money, compulsively stashing and investing and then "righteously" live on ridiculously low "poverty level" incomes. Ironically, these kinds of people become haughty in their humility.

Money is scarce

This is a very subtle attitude about money that at first glance appears to be quite honorable. We fear that once the money we have now is spent, that's it, there will be no more. Those who have lived through the Depression or depression-like times are prone to this type of thinking and refuse to let it go. Sometimes our learned fears offer us a sick kind of security blanket. If you fear the future, inflation, the ever-increasing cost-of-living, and also that money is scarce, you have the makings of an impossible situation. You have made yourself a victim of a scarcity that does not exist.

Left alone, feelings of deprivation and negative thinking quickly become self-fulfilling prophecies. If you are convinced that money is scarce and good things will never come your way, that's exactly what's going to happen, guaranteed. Because you are convinced things will never change you unconsciously repel any good which might be trying to flow into your life. I believe this is the attitude which perpetuates dependence on welfare, generation after generation after generation. Children reared in this type of environment see the system as their only alternative and through self-fulfilling prophecy make sure scarcity is their destiny and that of their children and their children's children and on and on.

Money can buy love and approval

We don't actually think about it or verbalize it, but that is exactly what we are attempting to do when we overspend and get into debt to buy for others. We justify our outlandish spending because we are acting out of benevolence, i.e., "I'm buying for others."

When we go on a never-ending quest to please others, trying to win their approval through constantly buying and giving we are reflecting our own feelings of unworthiness. We desperately want others to approve and love us in order to fill up the huge void left by our inability to find approval within ourselves.

We are looking to buy love and approval when we are compelled to take the biggest and best gift to the party or throw the biggest and best birthday party for the children. We feel we are buying status by picking up the tab at the restaurant, by leasing a new luxury car, or wearing expensive clothes. There is an element of good feeling too, when we can make others envious. We derive some kind of sick pleasure from the jealousy we can create in others. We are driven to do all of these crazy things in order to feel the personal approval we can find nowhere else.

We give power to money

We do not think of money in the same way we do other things that we own. For instance we would never think of worshiping our refrigerators or having a love affair with our patio furniture. Possessions like these certainly contribute to our well-being and happiness but we would never hold them responsible for it. We don't lose sleep worrying that the stereo or personal computer will ruin us, and we don't live for the day that we might be lucky enough for them to give us power and provide our security. But money? We do not treat money as the inanimate object that it is. We treat money as something with superior power that "happens" to us if we are lucky enough or good enough. We worship it, have love affairs with it, blame it, hate it, dream about it, live for it, curse it, pray for more of it, sacrifice our families for it, hand over control of our lives to it, sell our souls for it, and wind up in bondage to it. It is our best friend and our worst enemy. We can't live with it but we can't live without it. But don't despair; you can change.

You can change

It is possible to transform the way you feel about money. In fact, this is the first and most important step in this Money Makeover. It is a mandatory step because learning new methods for handling money without first going back to discover the basis for your bad ones would be as ridiculous as patching a flat tire with a Band-Aid.

I am confident that whether you compulsively hoard money, are incomeless, are slightly uncomfortable financially, are buried in debt despite your impressive income, or have just filed for bankruptcy —unless you are willing to confront your basic money beliefs—things probably will never change for you. Whatever your present situation, it will only get worse. History simply will repeat itself. It doesn't matter whether you've sought help for your money situation, tried every newfangled budget, or been through formal credit counseling and know more about money management than The Donald himself (which might indicate you're in really big trouble). The fact that you are with me at this particular moment leads me to believe you may have failed to deal with the real issues.

I have a feeling that this time is going to be different because finally you are going to discover the root issues, the reasons you are at this point in your financial life. We are going to uncover the beliefs which cause you to operate the way you do. You will have an opportunity to make the necessary fundamental changes to become a wise and trustworthy caretaker of your finances. Exciting, isn't it?

You need money, not necessarily more money

I wouldn't even think of trying to convince you that you don't need money. Of course you need money. All of us need money. But contrary to what you've always assumed, more money is not the answer to your financial difficulties. If it were, you would not be in your present situation. Think about it. Don't you make much more money today than you did say, 10 years ago? But it just never seems to be enough, does it? Exactly how long have you been waiting for the nebulous "more money?" Contrary to your fondest dreams, financial ease will never be achieved by getting more money. The answer is in learning how to make better use of what you do have.

Money is not . . .

The truth is that money is not power, pleasure, freedom, happiness, security, or choices. Rather it is a completely neutral commodity for which we trade our life's energy, skills, or abilities. Money cannot make us happy, it cannot ruin us, it cannot make us powerful, and it cannot insure a hassle-free life. Money has no power on its own. However, what we do with our money, the way that we behave with our money, can produce power, pleasure, freedom, happiness, security, and choices. Money is not important but options are and money bestows options. Options have a genuine and positive effect on our happiness and quality of life.

You are your attitudes

Because what we believe shapes who we are, who we are is revealed in our attitudes and our attitudes determine our behavior. If false beliefs produce bad behavior, it makes sense that replacing them with truth will produce good behavior. Left undetected a false belief system will result in negative attitudes and therefore inappropriate and destructive behavior.

Your money behavior is a direct reflection of your money beliefs. Your money beliefs, true or false, are the driving force behind your every financial act. It doesn't matter where those beliefs came from. The way to be cured of your money ills is to uncover and eliminate false money beliefs and replace them with beliefs based in truth and wisdom. Proper attitudes and appropriate behavior will naturally follow. Basing your life in truth will result in a return of choice, sanity, personal dignity, and solvency.

Solvency simply means being comfortable with the money that you have. Solvency is that confident feeling of being prepared for any circumstance, of living with joy and peace, of living within your means at all times.

Since my divorce everyone remarks what a great job I am doing as a single mother of two teens. We have a nice home, nice car, I work full-time, etc. The secret is I have been putting things I can't afford (just about everything!) on my credit cards.

It began with giving too much to my children out of guilt over the divorce, pretending we could still have a large home and wanting to make up for years of few clothes, activities, and meals out while married to someone who splurged on his male toys (guns, guitars, beer, tools) while we lived frugally. But did it dawn on me to cut back in order to pay these new debts off? No. My daughter had problems with friends and her dad was ignoring her so I tried to ease her pain with clothes, meals out, and favorite foods at home. The debt grew. When her brother visited I tried to bribe him with favorite expensive foods, movies, meals out. Soon gas and groceries went on the card.

The spending continued as I was often too exhausted after a lengthy commute to cook at home —more meals out. I followed a course in budgeting and set up a budget, but again exhausted and stressed, the spending continued until that magical day I was browsing in a bookstore and came upon your book.

I feel like I have come out of the closet, admitting I have a real emotional problem with my spending. I am beginning to understand why I am overspending, and I have begun to recognize these feelings that surface when I am tempted to try to ease my children's emotional pain and my own unorganized stressful life by overspending.

I have begun making some major changes in the way I spend. I no longer feel I must indulge my children with expensive things in order to make up to them for the pain they have gone through.

Last weekend I baked my daughter's birthday cake —the first scratch cake I've made in years. She was so impressed that I'd "gone to all that trouble for her!"

My eyes have been opened to the root of my financial woes (not the divorce, not teens, not working full time, not the "high cost of things")— the problem is me and my attitudes about money. You have given me courage and support. Thank you.

Elizabeth

I need help in order to save myself from myself! I am a spending addict.

Would you believe I earn $50,000 a year and live from paycheck to paycheck? A few months ago I bought ninety-five [cosmetic] products, although I'm allergic to cologne. A year ago I bought six men's watches and had to search my brain cavity to think of people to give them to. A clear indication that my addiction has worsened is that I used to buy for myself. Now I buy stuff and have to find people to give the items to. My closets and garage are loaded with packed boxes.

A trip to a store is financial roulette for me. I never know what or how much I will buy.

Alysha

I wanted to share with you a bit of success I have experienced recently. One night several weeks ago I left work totally stressed, seriously considering submitting my resignation. Instead of going home to a dark and lonely house I decided to stop at a favorite department store to "unwind."

I wasn't looking for anything in particular when I just happened on this fabulous suit. It fit perfectly and was drop-dead gorgeous but the $400 price tag was nearly half my weekly gross income.

I can't believe I did it, but I went to the credit department and actually asked if they could increase my credit limit because I really felt like I deserved it after all I'd been through. They did.

I left with the most beautiful suit I've ever seen and nearly floated out to the car. As I opened the door I tried really hard not to think about the fact I'm two car payments behind or that I didn't even have two bucks to my name to buy dinner. Believe it or not I am making progress because six months ago I wouldn't have even thought about the car payments or my pitiful cash position. . . .

Thanks to you I had the most miserable weekend of my life. I know that debt is killing me and if I keep adding to it I am doing nothing but mortgaging my future and any options I might hope to have.

I think I tried that darned suit on 50 times, justifying all the reasons I needed to have it: I deserved it, it would enhance my career, it would last forever, it made me feel good. You name it, I came up with it.

The following Monday I did a most difficult thing. I returned it. Once the return transaction was completed I got this burst of confidence, walked up to the credit department, took out my charge card, cut it in half, kindly explained to the teller that I can no longer accept credit in this store and asked that my account be closed. They were very nice and did not strip me of my dignity as I might have imagined.

That suit has taught me so much about myself. The pleasure I can create by spending is nearly addictive.

Rachel

. . . my childhood training convinced me I was undeserving and incompetent. My 18-year marriage cemented that belief. I believed women don't do money, artists can't do math, money is beyond my comprehension, finances are too confusing, someone else will have to do it.

. . . I am sometimes overcome with the pain of remembered deprivation, never any money, wearing hand-me-downs all through school, sometimes not enough to eat and mostly barefoot.

The fear of deprivation somehow played a major role in my need to spend. As long as I had credit I didn't have to think about money. Instead I looked around for ways to improve my life with money; the first credit I used was to furnish my home. Next, I dressed myself and my children beautifully. I improved the value of my property at every opportunity. I felt like Cinderella, and I shopped compulsively.

Since my financial crisis developed last year I have been aware of a growing sense of shame and the need to do something about it.

I have worked out a way to regain the power and management of my life and money. I have worked out a budget that is clear to me. I am setting boundaries and learning to manage money. I am resolved to live within my income. I have no experience with this. I am charting a new course and feel uncertain and apprehensive.

I am reclaiming my right to be responsible for my life and money. I am determined, devoted and committed. . . .

Manon

CHAPTER 6

Developing Healthy Money Attitudes

I think addiction to spending money is just another manifestation of the dysfunctionality of our society as a whole and I am so relieved to have a program with concrete steps to take back my power and peace of mind.

Carolyn

Regardless of your present financial situation, regardless of the subtle or subconscious roles money has played in your life—you are not destined to live one more day under the control of your current money attitudes.

The way that you have handled your money up to this time is probably the result of learned behaviors. I don't know about you, but I received absolutely no education on the simple matter of money and its role in my life, so it's no wonder I just played it by ear and did what came naturally.

Now you have a choice. You can either continue with the bad habits which have landed you in need of a Money Makeover or you can replace them with new effective and far more appropriate attitudes. You have the opportunity to do just that by consciously choosing to change your attitudes and by replacing bad habits with new, healthy ones. New habits can be created the very same way that you established the old, destructive ones: by repeating specific actions over and over again until they become automatic responses. It takes just three weeks, twenty-one short days, to create a new habit and another three weeks to establish it for a lifetime.

Every attitude toward money which you read about in the previous chapter is wrong and destructive. We should not worship money, allow it to determine our self-worth, use it as an antidepressant, attempt to elevate ourselves by making others jealous with it, or fall prey to any of the other crazy ways in which money controls us.

Let me make this perfectly clear: No matter how much you feel dominated by money, no matter how addicted you think you are to your credit cards and to overspending—you have the ability to stop this outrageous behavior. You are not powerless over money's force in your life.

As a bright and capable human being you have a powerful brain which elevates you above all other creatures. You have the ability to make choices and to control your actions. And you can change your actions anytime you set your mind to it. By repeating a new action over and over again, you will change your attitudes. And when your attitudes change, your behavior changes and the new action becomes automatic.

As your attitudes about money change something remarkable will happen. You will allow yourself to accept abundance and enjoy financial ease—not necessarily wealth, but financial ease. You will see the focus of your life change from financial chaos to serenity and fulfillment.

Following are nine healthy attitudes about money. I have written them in the first-person so that as you read them, they immediately become personal.

New Attitude # 1: I choose to understand the truth about money.

I know that money is not love, happiness, a deity, evil, worth, respect, social standing, approval, acceptance, or goodness, nor can it purchase any of these things for me.

Money is simply a valuable commodity for which I exchange my abilities, skills, and talents. Money provides a means to a worthy end for me and my family. I can abuse money, or I can use it to provide privileges and options. I acknowledge that as these flow into my life my responsibility will increase because to whom much is given, much is required.

Now that I've got it through my thick head exactly what money can and cannot do I am freed up to find genuine and lasting sources of happiness, joy, approval, peace, and goodness. Wow, what a feeling!

New Attitude # 2: I commit to honesty.

I acknowledge that writing checks before the funds are in my account, purchasing on credit knowing that I don't have the resources to repay the debt immediately, misleading my creditors, failing to balance my checking account, not paying my taxes, not working up to my abilities, ignoring my bills, hiding my purchases, and concealing my debts from my spouse are some of the ways that I have practiced dishonesty in the past. I commit to a new way of life, one of total integrity where I refuse to spend more money than I have. Now I will respond openly and honestly in all of my financial affairs.

New Attitude # 3: I will not spend money which is not mine.

I commit to incur no more unsecured debt. I won't borrow from a friend, accept a service that I will pay for later, take a loan from a bank, charge anything on any credit card which cannot be repaid immediately, or in any way pledge future income for present goods and services. No one can force me to debt one more cent.

New Attitude # 4: I will respond appropriately.

In the past I have used money inappropriately to reverse bad moods, kill the pain of disappointment, make up for losses, feed my empty heart, fill my loneliness, anesthetize my sadness, and gain love and approval. Not only have I failed to deal with the real issues in my life, I have ended up with a pile of debts.

From now on when I encounter a season of discouragement, a period of stress, moments of disappointment, or terms of loneliness, I will not spend my way through in an effort to avoid facing the real problem. Instead I will face the situation head on and employ appropriate ways which will cause me to grow and will not put my solvency at risk.

New Attitude # 5: I accept the responsibility and reject the shame.

I acknowledge that I am responsible for my present financial situation. I have made some mistakes. I have failed to plan ahead appropriately. But I am not the sum of my debts; my bank balance does not define who I am and my creditors do not own me. I owe them money which I will repay, but I do not owe them my life. No matter how painful or troubled my past has been, it is my past. I am now dealing with the future and joyfully I press on, looking forward to solvency.

New Attitude # 6: I commit to clarity.

I acknowledge that because I have no idea where my money goes I have allowed it to disappear. As part of my process toward solvency I commit to record the simple details of how my money is spent. I commit to facing the truth on a daily basis by keeping my purchases recorded, my checkbook perpetually balanced, my mail opened, and my bills in order and paid on time.

New Attitude # 7: I will exercise my dreams.

This is my life. It is not a dress rehearsal. I refuse to defer living life to its fullest until some future time when I get my money situation straightened out. Without my dreams my recovery will be bleak at best. I am confident that combining my life's work with my dreams will be a source of genuine happiness and, in turn, will bring success.

New Attitude # 8: I will search out true sources of happiness and will practice thankfulness.

I acknowledge that true happiness is found in those infinitely precious things that may not be stolen from me. I will look for my joy and contentment in that which is permanent, and I will find my anchor in the fact that the God of the universe loves and cares for me. As I see the bigger picture my day-to-day money issues will diminish and pale in the light of what is truly important.

I know it is impossible to feel self-pity and thankfulness at the same time. The best way I can let go of worry and self-pity is to practice thankfulness.

I will create my own personal and specific thankfulness list. I will begin thinking in terms of my blessings which money cannot buy like the freedoms I enjoy and the health with which I've been blessed.

My thankfulness list will become something permanent and precious in my life. During the down times (which will inevitably visit me from time to time because I am human and that happens to everybody) I will reach for my constantly growing thankfulness list instead of the credit cards.

New Attitude # 9: I am committed to do whatever it takes and make whatever sacrifices are necessary to achieve and maintain solvency.

I understand that desperate situations often require drastic measures. I am willing to make those adjustments necessary to live within my means.

. . . this is how I feel: I am serving a jail sentence. I was lured into a cage not knowing what I was getting into but I felt proud to be there. As soon as I lost control the cage locked. Now I'm serving my time. I have great behavior, but my creditors changed the locks. I'm trying to get out, but the creditors will see to it that I stay in and pay a much higher price than I think is fair. I'm their prisoner and that was never the deal. The finance charge is my guard and he carries a machine gun attempting to kill my hope and my dreams. But at least in my jail cell a ray of sun shines upon me. For I know, when my sentence is up, without having escaped or letting anyone bail me out, I shall never return and my wisdom and experience have already set me free.

Lori

Thank you for paving the way for all of us who need this kind of lifestyle. I greatly enjoyed your book and have started to put some of your advice to work. I think the most important change, though, is the way my thinking about money has changed.

We recently went to a large community garage sale and bought about $200 worth of almost new baby clothes and toys for about $30. The best part was getting to brag about our 'cheapskatism' later at a dinner party.

We never would have considered buying second hand before but this way of living is finally very socially acceptable, and we know it's the right thing for us to do. My wife has agreed to read your book next and we both are committed to changing our financial picture FOREVER!!

John

I am a young mother and very busy domestic engineer working part-time outside the home as well. I got into a real pickle living beyond my true means and had to take drastic action. Once the bells went off and I started buckling down, the need to just plain spend money for the sake of spending money wasn't appealing. Rather like being an alcoholic, I made a personal commitment (cold turkey!) to quit credit spending. It took me 18 months to pay off everyone and during that time I also SAVED a small amount, too, to (as you say) keep my attitude well adjusted. During the next six months I saved to take a little trip, and when I returned I was tan and feeling on top of the world. I had licked the evil forces.

It's harder now to not slip back into an anxiously planned occasional compulsive purchase or two. I realize my compulsion kicks in at times, and I have to really dig deep for that willpower.

It's not so much keeping up with anyone, it's more

like living without the things you "think" you want in your life. The fact is, you cannot have everything, and it's a well managed household that comfortably attains all their needs . . . and plans ahead for the high priority wants.

Gail

CHAPTER 7

Money Makeover:
The Basics

The secret of achieving your permanent Money Makeover is in finding balance and then maintaining it for the rest of your life. Any financial difficulties you are experiencing now are a result of one basic thing: imbalance. The greater your money problems—the more out of balance you are.

Strange as it sounds, if you are ever going to achieve financial freedom you must come under the authority of certain universal and unchanging financial principles which, when put into practice, will bring the kind of freedom you've only dreamed of in the past.

In a way, I wish I could take credit for the principles which follow (they're that good). Funny thing about truth, it never fails. It is as reliable today as it was two thousand, maybe even two million, years ago.

What follow are the basic Money Makeover principles. If you will apply these rules to your life systematically as explained and outlined in the following chapters, your life will be changed forever.

Money Makeover Step #1: Part of everything you earn is yours to keep. This is the Principle of *Saving*.

Money Makeover Step #2: Part of everything you earn is yours to give away. This is the Principle of *Giving*.

Money Makeover Step #3: You must have a Freedom Account. This is the Principle of *Preparation*.

Money Makeover Step #4: You must have a Rapid Debt Reduction Plan. This is the Principle of *Living Debt-free*.

Money Makeover Step #5: Your lifestyle must fit within the boundaries of your income. This is the Principle of *Restraint*.

These are the basic principles around which we will design your personal Money Makeover. If you plan to ignore any of them you might as well consider your present situation the best it will ever be. Don't forget that your financial problems are a result of having ignored one or more of these fundamental principles.

. . . when we married he had 10 credit cards and I had three. We both had good jobs, he in banking and I in marketing. We decided to wait to start a family so we spent and spent and spent. We traveled all over the world and spent even more. As my husband became a senior vice president our credit lines were increased tremendously. We had, within the first five years of our marriage, every credit card known to man. I would get so excited when at least twice a month we'd get an already-approved card from somewhere. I bought when I felt good, and I bought when I felt bad. The idea of paying off a credit card never occurred to either of us. We were paying more than the minimum required payment each month, but not much. Every time we got to the limit they almost always raised it. I felt great. I spent a fortune on clothes. My husband spent a fortune on art and diamonds.

When we decided we needed a house we had no savings so we borrowed on our credit cards. We even applied for two new ones so we'd have enough. We bought a beautiful house in Mill Valley, an exclusive suburb of San Francisco.

In 1988 my husband's bank went through a major reorganization. He was laid off along with quite a few of his friends. It didn't seem that bad. They were all given a "golden parachute" (lots of perks and money upon leaving). He wanted to take a month off to decide what to do. The bank raised the interest on the credit cards, but they increased our limits by $2,000 on each line of credit just so we wouldn't feel so badly about the increase in interest. Crazy, isn't it?

My husband was getting job offers but said he wasn't ready. I was traveling at the time with my job, and figured he was going through burn-out.

Within the next six months he started a company with two friends. They put up their retirement accounts for the capital. Five months later the company folded.

I managed to keep my job even though my company was going through a major shake-up, and the problem of living on one income was beginning to be a real problem. So we handled it the way we handled every problem: we borrowed against our credit cards.

Within six months we were in a terrible financial disaster. It was a problem just to make the house payments. My husband was in a severe depression and said he just couldn't take it anymore. He left me and moved in with his mother. Two months later he asked for a divorce. When I inquired what his plans were for all the bills he informed me he just couldn't deal with them; besides, his doctor had ordered a stress-free environment.

I sat down on New Year's Day and gathered all my bills together. The total was $78,156.37, most of it at 19 percent interest. My annual salary was about $40,000. I had a $3,400 monthly house payment, and I could no longer borrow on my credit cards. Two cards had been turned over to collection agencies and at this point I couldn't pay the minimum on anything.

I decided to sell the house and with my half of the net proceeds ($5,250) put a security deposit on an apartment and saved enough to cover three months rent.

I had creditors calling all the time, so I made a list of who I owed and began calling them. I knew I had to do it all in one day or I would never get up the nerve again. Before I called I made a schedule of repayments I could handle. Most creditors would not accept less than the minimum. Luckily one of my biggest creditors listened to my story. They checked how we had been paying the bill and found we'd not

been late in eight years. They told me to let them know when I could start making payments, and they would rewrite the loan so it wouldn't show up negative on my credit report. I didn't even care about my credit report! But this gave me some much needed breathing room. The other creditors were not so kind.

Most collection agencies said they would only extend my payments for 10 months. I told them that if I couldn't make the minimum, I sure couldn't pay off the entire amount in 10 months! They all wrote me horrible letters and said vicious things on the phone. But I just didn't have the money, so I kept paying them—according to my schedule.

A year later a collection agency sent me a letter stating that they would settle one account for 50 percent if I paid within fourteen days. I called them and said I'd try. I had been storing most of my furniture so I thought I might be able to come up with it by selling my furniture and piano. The settlement was for $3,200 on a $6,400 balance. I had a big garage sale to liquidate all the stuff we had amassed and sold the furniture. I came up with the $3,200 sent it to them immediately and promptly received a letter stating that debt was paid!

Next I picked the five highest interest rate bills and decided to work on them while making nominal payments to the others. Even coming up with the gas money to get to work was a challenge. I had $70 a month for food. We'd spent more than that per meal when we ate out before my world crashed in on me. I hated myself, felt sorry for myself, but was mostly totally bewildered by how this could happen. I'd never been a murderer or anything really bad. It just wasn't fair!

When I started paying things off I had 29 creditors. The minute one would get paid off I would start on another one. There were so many bills and so many phone calls and letters I never felt better when anything was paid. I am grateful to your book and newsletter for helping me see I could be happy about even one zero balance.

I began to see the headway I was making on my debts. It was very slow—all I did was pay bills. I even got up enough nerve to call a creditor and offer a settlement! I owed $1500 and offered them $750. They took it.

A great aunt shocked me when she left me a little house in the middle of nowhere and a 15-year-old car in her will. I was warned the house was not livable. A local real estate agent told me I could get about $17,000 for it. But my total outstanding bills were $53,976.11! He told me it would bring $35,000 if fixed up. I'd never done anything like that, but I decided to fix it up!

I sold everything I had left including my jewelry and video equipment. I went to pawn shops and estate jewelry buyers as part of my campaign to liquidate everything I could. Since I'd been laid off by this time, moving to Nowhere, USA, seemed liked the best thing to do.

I turned my leased car over to an agency which took over the payments (which turned out to be a big mistake and a whole different story), put a new battery in the 15-year-old wreck and had it serviced. I found a job with a local contractor ($30,000 annually), but with no rent and no car payments I was way ahead.

I have paid off all of the bills but two. I have completely remodeled and updated the house without any hired help. I just didn't have the money! I have totally replaced all the wiring, plumbing, and fixed the gas. I did everything with the books I borrowed from the library. I am a firm believer in

Sunset books! Everything has passed city inspection. I've pulled up flooring down to the sub-floor and replaced studs. I'm great with dry-wall and replacing ceilings. I'm almost finished with the outside renovation—and have two offers on the house! I should clear around $30,000 which should be enough to pay off all of my remaining debts.

I know that financial disaster was inevitable for us, but it was unbelievably difficult for me to admit. I felt ashamed without my credit cards. I loved using them! Somehow, they made me who I wanted to be. I now know that this kind of thinking is totally false.

I believe the problem my husband and I had with debting cost us our marriage, my husband's self-worth, and the children I always wanted. I don't think it will ever be safe for me to use a credit card again.

Friends often ask me why I just didn't declare bankruptcy. I chose to find a way to repay the debts not for self-punishment but in a way to give myself back some personal value.

For the past five years I have done nothing but pay off bills. I have paid back a great deal of money! The kindness of my great aunt was luck beyond anything I could have imagined. Not having to pay rent or car notes truly super-charged my repayment plan.

I still get sick when I think of the money we wasted, the opportunities we missed. I have learned a great deal about myself.

I am currently in the process of being transferred back to California. My ex-husband is still living with his mother and to this day has never held another job.

I hope something in my story might help someone else. Your newsletter helps me keep going. I still get the urge to splurge . . . but I don't!

Eileen

CHAPTER 8

Insuring Your Future Income: The Principle of Saving

"The peace of mind that comes with saving even that small amount of money is immeasurable!"

Leona and Hart

You must save for the future. Part of everything you earn is yours to keep—not to save up so you can buy a new sofa or remodel the kitchen—but yours to keep so that it will grow and multiply and care for you in the future. Think of it this way: Properly managed, money you save will bear children, and grandchildren, and even great-grandchildren!

Right now you may be throwing up your hands and writing me off as a total idiot who thinks you can save money you don't even have.

People in financial difficulty don't have a formal savings program. Of course not, because everyone knows "you save whatever you have left over" and those of us in financial trouble never have anything left over! Not so hard to figure. After all, we are so busy spending next month's money on last month's bills that the thought of saving anything hardly crosses our minds.

Saving is something we'll do someday when we win the lottery. It's something we'll do someday when we have $2,000 extra to get started. Someday, someday, someday.

A part of everything you earn is yours to keep. When you look at your paycheck, do you get a sick feeling in the pit of your stomach because it is so small and every stinkin' cent is spoken for? Well, my friend, that's going to change. Your goal is *eventually* to save 10 percent of everything you earn. Can you really do it? You bet you can!

Your savings plan needs to be formal and consistent. *Formal* means a predetermined, fixed amount. It can be 50 cents or 50 dollars. I don't care where you start, but it has to be the same amount every time. "Consistent" means the same time every week, every two weeks, every month, or whatever. If you save a set amount at a set time, then you have a formal and consistent savings program.

Studies show that anyone with an annual income of $10,000 or more has *some* discretionary money. That's it. You have no more excuses. For you, saving money is indeed a choice. You can choose to or choose not to. But you can no longer say you can't.

The best way to save is to have the money automatically moved into your savings account. This can be done through payroll deduction or through your bank which will take money from your checking account and deposit it into your savings.

A part of everything you earn is yours to keep. That just has to be one of the sweetest sentences in the English language. I need to keep repeating it because you need to keep hearing it. Notice: I said "yours to keep." To keep!

Eventually this savings program is going to start growing for you, just like a tiny seed that when planted, watered, and cared for will multiply and multiply and multiply and grow strong, secure, and mighty. The roots of your "savings tree" will be deep, and you will feel protected.

If you dare, think about all the interest you've paid on your debts and how much more you're going to have to pay before you become debt-free. Kinda' makes you sick, doesn't it? Think of applying that same principle to what you are going to save. It works the same way but feels a whole lot better.

Example: Jerry begins a formal and consistent savings program on his twenty-first birthday. He saves $50 each month. If he earns only 6 percent interest during his working years his $26,400 total investment will grow to $129,859 by the time he retires. If the same amount earns an average of twelve percent interest (certainly not unthinkable), he'd have $960,949. Of course he will owe tax on the interest somewhere along the line, but that's still almost a million dollars thanks to the miracle of compounded interest.

Interest rates rise and fall just like mountain highways. If you get discouraged when rates drop into the "valley" and decide two or three percent interest is just not worth the trip, you may never experience the breathtaking "mountain top" experiences. Don't forget you are in this for the long-haul. It is the average rate of interest compounded over a long period of time which will secure your future and calm your fears.

If you have a financial calculator or are a mathematical whiz, calculate what the miracle of compounded interest would do if you were to save 10 percent of your annual income starting now until you retire. Here's an example: If your average annual income is $50,000 and you save 10 percent ($5,000) each year in an investment that earns 10 percent interest compounded for 35 years, your nest egg will become $1,595,115 before taxes, even though you will contribute only $175,000. And that does not take into consideration any raises you will get over 35 years. It's a miracle, folks.

You've experienced the devastating growth rate of debts. You know how interest has compounded against you and landed you under a mountain of anxiety. Well, it's time you see the miracle of compounded interest when it is growing in your favor. The secret to the miracle of compounded interest is in saving consistently, every week, every month. Slow growth is the key. This miracle is available to anyone. And if you can't start with 10 percent, start with 10 dollars, or 10 cents. Just start.

While the sugar bowl in the cupboard might be a good place to stash the cash in the beginning, I don't recommend that approach for very long. Because many banks have ridiculous fees and minimums on regular savings accounts, before you rush out and open an account make sure you know the rules. If you can find an account that will cost you nothing so long as you make very few withdrawals, go for it. Check to see if your bank has a school account or student program. Usually these accounts require no minimums and have no fees but still pay interest on the account. Open the account in your child's name, but make sure you control it. You don't want to make withdrawals except to reinvest. Also, many credit unions have no-fee savings accounts. Set up an automatic savings withdrawal from your checking account. Remember, money you don't see you don't miss.

Get into the habit of feeding the account regularly, but don't get into the habit of checking on it every week. It's like the watched pot that never boils. The benefit to you right now is not in the balance in your bank book but in the new attitude you've developed. You've made a 180 degree change in the direction you were heading!

When you are putting something away for yourself, choosing to deny yourself in another area won't seem so unreasonable.

Once you start saving money expect to experience several things. Whereas previously you felt naked, scared, and vulnerable to life's curve balls, you will soon begin to feel more secure and protected. Putting money away in a bank or investment account may be the most addictive thing you've ever done. Save a little and you want to save more. Saving makes you feel like you're getting a handle on life. You begin to feel responsible and able to cope because you have better "vision." You are not stuck in the moment but instead are able to see the big picture and how your savings will give you security in the future. Saving money promotes maturity and self-discipline. It really does have a snowball effect. Saving money on a consistent basis is probably the best antidote to out-of-control spending and the best gift you will ever give yourself.

. . . I am carrying the burden of the knowledge of my debt in secrecy from my husband. He knows that I worry constantly about money and having enough for retirement. He has no idea how bad things are. The guilt and stress is killing me. . . .

Catherine

. . . you said to save at least 10 percent of your income for the future. I just started last June and my husband and I now have over $3,000 socked away. I put the money in a savings account we never touch.

I really, really want to thank you because while I've always been a good saver we've always spent with the best of them, too and this 10 percent off the top prevents us from frittering away all our extra money. . . .

Sue

. . . I had a very hard time accepting the idea of paying yourself first. We always kept waiting for the extra money so we could start saving but somehow it never seemed to come. Last month we said "Okay, no matter what we are taking 50 dollars and putting it into savings." With overtime we were able to save $300 last month. I'm so excited. . . .

Diane

CHAPTER 9

You Will Reap What You Sow: The Principle of Giving

I can't explain it, but I truly believe that there is an invisible reservoir of abundance in the universe that flows to those who observe the spiritual law of giving.

There is something about giving that can't be explained in purely rational terms. Giving seems to put a person in touch with his spiritual nature. Giving attracts money. Not a lot of money, necessarily, but enough to meet the giver's needs.

I know that some people are born with more caring personalities, but that's not what I'm talking about. The kind of giving which is part of your Money Makeover is purposeful, without regard for result or consequence. Regardless of one's personality type, this kind of giving can be easily learned.

If you've never been one to practice the art of "giving back," get ready to experience a whole new dimension in your life. I don't know of anything that will take your eyes off your own situation faster than giving to others.

You will always reap what you sow. That's true about everything from tending a vegetable garden to building relationships. And when it comes to your money, a tightfisted attitude gives nothing and receives nothing in return. But the truly generous person cannot "outgive." The more that flows out the more flows back.

I don't suggest that you should ever give in order to receive. True giving is done with no strings attached, no expectations of accolades, thank you notes, or returned favors. Unless you can give unconditionally, your giving will be nothing but manipulation.

How much should you give? The answer to that question is exactly the same as the answer to the following question: How much would you like to be blessed? You decide! Most everything I have ever studied agrees that ten percent is a good number. Don't panic; if you can't start with that, start with *something*.

Because giving is both an attitude and an action, don't ignore the fact you can give of your time and your talents in addition to your money to someone or to some responsible organization that needs them more than you.

This idea of active thankfulness may be something very new to you. The first thing you should do is compose a Thankfulness List. Start writing down the things for which you are thankful. Make this a perpetual list—one that you add to from time to time and with which you become so familiar you could recite it from memory. Practicing thankfulness on a daily basis will change your life. Your eyes will be turned from yourself to others. You'll find your feelings of self pity will diminish, your relationships will be enhanced, and your stress level will decline. You'll experience a natural desire to express that thankfulness. Giving will be the result. You won't be able to stop yourself.

As an important part of your Money Makeover, a portion of everything you earn and everything you are should be given back in some way.

Giving out of your abundance is an act of thanksgiving but giving out of your need is an act of faith. When you are the neediest is when you should give the most!

. . . Back in 1930 I was a young married minister, in Syracuse, New York. My salary which had been a handsome $6000 (in those days) a year was cut twice —first to $5000, then to $4000. We had no manse or home supplied by the church. Everyone was frightened and depressed. Businesses were failing. Nobody could borrow money; there was no money to be had. Men used to greet one another grimly by saying, "Have you had your pay cut yet?" Everyone had to take several cuts before that depression ended, and many people lost their jobs altogether.

With a salary of $4000 a year I just didn't see how we could get by. My salary was the only income we had. I was helping my younger brother with college expenses, and I knew he had to count on that. The pressure got worse and worse. I hated to burden Ruth [my wife] with my fears. One night I went out alone and walked through Walnut Park near our little apartment and for the first time in my life I felt icy terror clutching at my mind and heart. I was terrified. When I finally went home I said to Ruth, "We're in a desperate situation. We can't pay the bills. What are we going to do?" And her answer really startled me. She said, "We're going to start tithing."

"Tithing?" I echoed. "We can't! It's impossible!"

"Not impossible," Ruth said. "Essential. You know what the Old Testament promises to those who give 10 percent of everything to the Lord." I can see her yet, standing in the kitchen and quoting, "Bring ye all the tithes into the storehouse . . . and prove Me now herewith said the Lord of hosts, if I will not open you the windows of heaven and pour you out a blessing that there shall not be room enough to receive it." Mal. 3:10.

"We're going to do that," she said stoutly, "because tithing is an act of faith and the Bible says that if we have faith even as small as a grain of mustard seed nothing will be impossible for us. We have to start imaging God's prosperity."

So we did it. And Ruth was right. Money didn't pour in, but there always was enough. Furthermore, the act of tithing calmed my fears and stimulated my mind so that I began thinking. I started imaging. I knew I had one small talent: public speaking. And so I offered myself as a public speaker wherever one was needed. I spoke at civic clubs and garden clubs and graduations and community gatherings. Sometimes I was paid five or 10 dollars, sometimes nothing at all. But it helped. What a thrill I felt when I received the first $25 fee. Then someone who heard me speak offered me a chance to go on radio. Again, I received no money for this but the number of speaking invitations increased. So one thing led to another and gradually we began to get our heads above water.

I am convinced that tithing did it. Ruth and I have been tithers ever since. Through the years in sermons and talks I have recommended tithing to thousands of people and hundreds have been persuaded to try it. Of those hundred, not one has ever told me that the experiment failed, that he regretted it, or that it was a mistake. Not a single person.

It's almost as if there is an invisible reservoir of abundance in the universe that can be tapped if you will just obey certain spiritual laws. The word *abundance*, I'm told, comes from a Latin phrase meaning to "rise up in waves." When you tithe, it does seem as if little waves of abundance start rising up all around you.

So if you have financial difficulties, face up to them not just with courage and intelligence, but also with warmhearted generosity and concern for others.

Dr. Norman Vincent Peale

CHAPTER 10

Freedom Account: The Principle of Preparation

We are about to uncover what I am sure is a major source of your financial difficulties. I have read so many letters and talked to so many people about their financial situations that I have begun to see a pattern. To my utter amazement the majority of these people are simply repeating what happened to me—over and over again.

Most people learn to fit their regular monthly expenses into their average monthly income, getting by—not in an exemplary way perhaps, but getting by nonetheless.

Somehow the rent gets paid, food arrives on the table, the car payment is met, and the utility companies keep providing electricity, water, and gas.

Since monthly income covers these predictable monthly payments it is easy to get comfortable, to feel like everything is just peachy. So peachy, in fact that taking on a little extra debt (It's only $15 a month, dear!), making purchases with discretionary income, which we mistakenly define as anything that represents a balance in the checkbook, feels okay. It's okay to have a few extra dinners out because there are a few extra bucks in the checking account. It's okay to splurge here and there because it feels like there's enough money.

Without our noticing the monthly income and the regular monthly expenses have a way of becoming dangerously close. Given enough splurging there is less and less of a cushion in time. Occasional pay increases provide a better cushion but are quickly absorbed into thin air, or so it seems.

The problem is something I've named Selective Amnesia. It is a form of denial found far too often among those who can least afford such a malady.

Let's look at the symptoms of Selective Amnesia and their debilitating consequences. One symptom is being totally unaware that the car, for instance, is wearing out with every mile it is driven. We don't come right out and say it, but we live as though the tires are going to last forever, that *our* tires are the only ones on Planet Earth made from an indestructible material. Each month that we do not experience tire problems just confirms this mysterious but true fact. Since the car starts up every morning, doesn't leak oil, shifts gears flawlessly month after month we live as if it will always perform at this level of excellence.

When it comes to any kind of automobile maintenance beyond the ceremonial oil change, most people slip easily into Selective Amnesia. So what happens when those nondestructive tires on the family jalopy completely give up the ghost (all four of them at the same time, of course) and refuse to hold one more pound of air? Why, we fall apart bemoaning this "tragedy." Or how about when the brakes go through the rotors precisely at the same time you drop the tranny right there on the freeway? Oh no! Multiple and simultaneous crises! Oh my gosh! How can this family possibly endure another financial crisis?

And so it goes. Another opportunity to use the credit card rears its ugly head. But wait just one minute! Isn't that the legitimate purpose of credit cards? To handle all of life's little emergencies? Who cares about the interest rate or what this is going to do to our regular monthly expenses? The main thing is that the transaction gets approved. It doesn't even matter where the work is done so long as they accept the particular credit card we are able to produce.

What about that little thing called automobile insurance? While some pay this item monthly, many pay it quarterly, or semiannually. What a splendid opportunity for Selective Amnesia! As long as we don't see that bill coming in the mail every month, it couldn't possibly exist, could it? In a month when things are tight the last thing we need to think about is one twelfth of an annual insurance premium. Slipping into Selective Amnesia sure makes it easy to put off dealing with the matter until a more convenient time. Yeah, like when the red notice appears in the mail, you know, the one that says "cancellation no-tice" in giant type so big the postman couldn't pos-sibly miss it? Selective Amnesia allows us to gasp in horror upon its arrival. We act surprised and so in-nocent (as if we didn't see the three other notifica-tions that preceded it). "Oh, no, Harry! The car insurance is going to be canceled. Whatever will we do?"

So at the very last second, right before coverage is canceled at midnight, we do the all-American thing. We run to the bank for a cash advance, or call Mom and Dad, or write a hot check and hope to goodness that somehow we'll find a way to cover it. And if that doesn't work? Oh, just cancel the darned thing. We just can't afford it! Of course here again Selective Amnesia comes in quite handy because it allows us to completely forget that auto insurance is manda-tory in most states. Oh well, what else is one to do in the face of a "financial crisis?"

Most people ride a financial roller coaster month after month never knowing from one month to the next what new crisis will strike to knock them off their financial feet. And when a month ends with that roller coaster at the top of the hill we feel a false sense of financial ease. Whew! It feels so good to have all the bills paid. "Maybe we're finally getting ahead. Let's celebrate. We deserve it. Let's surprise the kids and put in a swimming pool."

Don't you wish you could find a way to plan ahead for life's inevitable emergencies? Don't you wish you could save for a vacation instead of running up the credit cards every year? Don't you wish you could have a little fun now and again, maybe indulge in a hobby or something other than work, work, work? Don't you wish you had the ability to keep all the bills paid and emergencies covered like those "rich" friends of yours? Don't you wish you could find a way to manage your resources in such a way so you could relax and be forever immune to Selective Amnesia?

Wish no more, because I'm going to help you get off the roller coaster. Can you imagine being able to plan ahead sufficiently to preclude getting hit again with an unexpected car repair bill or a huge property tax bill? Can you imagine getting through the holidays without feeling compelled to fall back on the plastic? Can you imagine having the ability to put aside funds for a new car *before* your current car falls apart right in front of the new car dealership? All of this will happen once you learn the cure for Selective Amnesia.

Meet the Freedom Account

Somehow you manage to pay your monthly rent or mortgage payment every month because past experience has taught you that failure to do so brings swift and painful consequences.

Imagine however, you are notified that effective immediately you will no longer pay rent (or the mortgage payment) each month, but will pay your rent for one year at a time. Your first yearly payment will be due one year from today.

Even though you aren't required to pay the rent each month, would you continue to see one twelfth of that annual payment as critical on a monthly basis as you now consider it? Probably not. More than likely rent would become one of your annual expenses which you hope will somehow take care of itself when the time comes.

Knowing yourself, what do you think your chances are of coming up with the, oh, let's say $12,000 annual payment one year from now? About as good as you having cash put away for most of your other intermittent expenses! It would be natural (not too smart but natural) for you to feel some relief knowing you will no longer have to deal with rent on a monthly basis. Some of us would actually experience a feeling of exhilaration calculating how this new arrangement will free up an "extra" $1,000 each month. Others (those who are breaking out in a cold sweat at this very moment) know the only right way to respond is to act as if one twelfth of the rent is still "due" every month and put that amount under the mattress or in a coffee can religiously on the first day of each month, come hell or high water. Very wise people would live no differently than if the rent were due every month.

Lest any of you get too used to such an insane idea, let me bring you back to reality. Your rent or mortgage payment is due every month just like it always has been. And one twelfth of your automobile maintenance is due every month along with one twelfth of your property taxes and one twelfth of quite a few things that you fail to consider on a monthly basis. Those expenses which you have but which are not paid monthly, are called *Irregular Expenses*.

Talk is cheap, isn't it? And there's no place it is cheaper than when it comes to saying you're going to start planning ahead for the irregular expenses. However, I am going to teach you a method which if followed diligently, will change your life forever. This is so exciting, so effective, so easy to handle, it borders on being miraculous. What follows is truly at the heart of turning your financial life around forever.

The key to achieving financial ease is in exerting control over your money. When you feel controlled by your financial situation you feel helpless and hopeless. But you can bring order and purpose to your personal finances by regularly setting aside funds in advance to cover your irregular expenses. Opening a Freedom Account will bring you a new sense of dignity, control and personal worth.

Setting Up a Freedom Account

Step 1. Determine Irregular Expenses. Using last year's check registers or paid bills' folder make a list of expenses *which you do not pay on a regular monthly* *basis.* These expenses might be paid quarterly, semi-annually, or annually. Multiply to reach an annual figure and then divide by 12 so you arrive at a figure which represents one twelfth of the total annual expense.

Here are some fictitious and hypothetical expenses Sam and Samantha Example, our fictitious and hypothetical sample family of four, calculated to be their irregular expenses. Please don't get hung-up on these dollar figures so that you miss the principles they represent. They are made-up and do not indicate what is normal or typical.

Auto maint./ repairs	$720/yr divided by 12 = $60/mo
Auto insurance	540/yr divided by 12 = $45/mo
Life insurance	480/yr divided by 12 = $40/mo
Property taxes	600/yr divided by 12 = $50/mo
Vacation	900/yr divided by 12 = $75/mo
Clothing	600/yr divided by 12 = $50/mo
	Total: $320/mo.

Sam and Samantha receive their income monthly, therefore they will handle their Freedom Account on a monthly basis. You may not be paid once a month, however since it would be impossible for me to convert every illustration to fit your particular payroll schedule I am assuming you will be able to translate the principles herein to fit your particular circumstances.

Step 2. Open two checking accounts. Yes, two. Shop for a bank or credit union which offers the best terms available such as no fee with a minimum balance, low-fee, or interest-bearing checking accounts with minimum balance. Open the two accounts at the same time and order checks (I highly recommend duplicate checks even though they cost a bit more) for each account. Have them personalized and add the words "Regular Account" and "Freedom Account" under your name and address, respectively. If you wish to continue using your present checking account for the "Regular Account" simply open a second at the same institution. The point is that you need to have *two active checking accounts at the same bank,* a bank that will offer you the very best terms and services. Do not, I repeat, do not accept an ATM card for this Freedom Account. Having ATM access to this account will defeat its purpose.

The Regular Account will continue to accommodate your monthly expenses and typical day-to-day needs such as groceries, gas, etc. You will continue to deposit your regular paychecks and other forms of income into this account.

Step 3. Request an automatic deposit authorization. At the time you open the accounts, request an automatic deposit authorization form (my bank calls this an "Automatic Money Transfer Form") instructing the bank to transfer the monthly total of your Irregular Expenses ($320 is the figure Sam and

Samantha will use) from your Regular Account into your Freedom Account on a specific day of the month, preferably no more than five days after the date on which you will be depositing your paycheck. *Example:* You are paid once a month on the 15th. You instruct the bank to automatically transfer $320 from your Regular Account into your Freedom Account on the 20th of every month. The five-day "cushion" will cover those unusual months when your regular payday falls on a holiday or weekend. The selection of your transfer date is very important because once established you can be sure the bank will never forget to make the transfer, nor will they be late.

Step 4. Get a looseleaf notebook and label it "Freedom Account." As far as the bank is concerned you have a single account which you have designated your Freedom Account. (Believe me, they couldn't care less how you refer to it; banks only recognize account numbers.) But you are going to treat it as six sub-accounts (or three, or eight as your particular case may be according to the number of Irregular Expenses you determined that you have; Sam and Samantha have six). Prepare one page per sub-account similar to Sam and Samantha's Auto Maint/Repair Account (Figure 10-1). Keep it simple. Fill in the title, enter the amount to be deposited into that particular sub-account in the upper right hand corner and prepare five columns,

"Date," "Transaction," "In," "Out," and "Balance" for each sub-account.

Step 5. Get in the habit. Each time you deposit your paycheck into your Regular Account, deduct the amount of your Irregular Expenses' monthly allocation ($320 for Sam and Samantha) on your Regular Account checkbook register. Don't even think about forgetting, the bank never will. It will feel weird in the beginning. You won't like making this debit entry because it feels like you're throwing away money. But no, you are *managing your money*. You are controlling your money instead of it controlling you.

Next, go to your Freedom Account notebook and enter the individual deposits. Here is how Sam and Samantha will make their first $320 automatic transfer deposit into their Freedom Account: They will enter a deposit of $75 into Auto Maint./Repair; $45 into Auto Insurance; $40 into Life Insurance; $50 into Property Taxes; $75 into Vacation and $50 into Clothing.

It is critical that in the first few months of this new behavior you do not give in to the temptation of withdrawing from your Freedom Account for anything other than the purpose of the sub-account. No borrowing. You may feel coerced, you'll be tempted, you'll be afraid you can't stop yourself, but don't. Please.

At times you will also be tempted to think of this account as a savings account and you may find your-

Freedom Account
Sam and Samantha Example

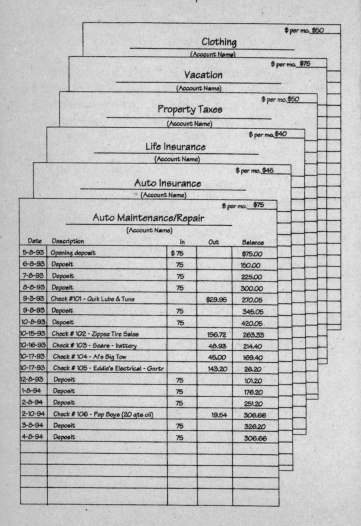

				$ per mo. $50
Clothing				
(Account Name)				

				$ per mo. $75
Vacation				
(Account Name)				

				$ per mo. $50
Property Taxes				
(Account Name)				

				$ per mo. $40
Life Insurance				
(Account Name)				

				$ per mo. $45
Auto Insurance				
(Account Name)				

$ per mo. $75

Auto Maintenance/Repair
(Account Name)

Date	Description	In	Out	Balance
5-8-93	Opening deposit	$ 75		$75.00
6-8-93	Deposit	75		150.00
7-8-93	Deposit	75		225.00
8-8-93	Deposit	75		300.00
9-3-93	Check #101 – Quik Lube & Tune		$29.95	270.05
9-8-93	Deposit	75		345.05
10-8-93	Deposit	75		420.05
10-15-93	Check # 102 – Zippee Tire Sales		156.72	263.33
10-16-93	Check # 103 – Sears – battery		48.93	214.40
10-17-93	Check # 104 – Al's Big Tow		45.00	169.40
10-17-93	Check # 105 – Eddie's Electrical – Gnrtr		143.20	26.20
12-8-93	Deposit	75		101.20
1-8-94	Deposit	75		176.20
2-8-94	Deposit	75		251.20
2-10-94	Check # 106 – Pep Boys (20 qts oil)		19.54	306.66
3-8-94	Deposit	75		326.20
4-8-94	Deposit	75		306.66

Fig. 10-1

self skipping your true savings or even hesitating to write appropriate payments out of the Freedom Account. This is not a savings account. This money has been committed already. The account will give new meaning to the phrase "ebb and flow." It is strictly a financial management tool. You have elevated yourself to a new category of maturity and financial responsibility. This is what financially responsible people do!

Next month you will repeat this same process. On the day you deposit your paycheck you will go right to your Regular Account checkbook register and deduct the automatic transfer. You will then go to your Freedom Account, enter the individual deposits and calculate the new balance for each of your sub-accounts. The total of all of your sub-accounts in this second month should be two twelfths of your annual irregular expenses. For Sam and Samantha it is $640, or $320 times two.

Continue this procedure every month. In the third or fourth month something wonderful will happen if you are diligent and DON'T GIVE UP. You will begin to experience a new level of comfort and tranquility. You will feel yourself start to relax and your previous compulsive purchasing activities will begin to disappear. You won't be driven to buy things in order to make yourself feel better because you will be fulfilling that need by being responsible and trustworthy with your finances.

Here's what happened to Sam and Samantha Example shortly after they set up their Freedom Account.

Sam had been trying to ignore a nagging guilt that he hadn't had the oil changed in the family car for way too long. They just didn't have the extra money or the free time necessary, and it became something easy to ignore. Some time during month four of their new Freedom Account it clicked in Sam's brain: Aha! Auto maintenance!

He ran to the Freedom Account notebook and found they had a balance of $300 in the Auto Maintenance/Repair sub-account (4 months × $75 = $300). He grabbed the Freedom Account checkbook, drove to Quik Lube 'n' Tune and asked for the $29.95 special. He entered $29.95 in the "Out" column of the Auto Maintenance/Repair sub-account page, wrote out check #101 and calculated the new balance, $270.05. He couldn't believe how good it felt. The Freedom Account had just worked.

Upon leaving work very late on October 14 Samantha was greeted by a flat tire. Rats! Just what she needed. Payday was still two weeks away, and she knew the spare was not in very good shape. All the way home she "sat light" because she was so nervous about riding on the spare. And she worried about how she and Sam were committed to incurring no new debt. But this was obviously an emergency. And then it hit her. Ah-ha! Auto maintenance. They'd become good managers of their money and this is exactly what they'd been preparing for! She arrived home with a smug grin on her face and scoured the newspaper to see what kind of sales she could find.

Early the following morning Sam headed for Zippee Tire Sales and purchased two new tires for $156.72. He wrote out check #102 and calculated the new balance of $263.33. It actually felt good!

Sam bounded out to the car that evening feeling pretty perky with those two new paid-for tires and all, got in, turned the key. Click, click, click and then NOTHING! Dead. Oh no! Who needs this? First the flat tire and now this! What else could possibly go wrong?!?

Not one to give up easily, Sam laid his head down on the steering wheel to gain a little composure and figure out what to do just as it dawned on him. Ah ha! Auto maintenance.

He walked a few blocks to Sears where he found a pretty good deal on a 48-month battery for $48.93. The Freedom Account can certainly handle this. What does he do? Check #103 is written to Sears for a new battery. He entered the transaction in the Freedom Account notebook on the Auto Maintenance/Repair page, calculated the new balance to be $214.40 and proceeded home, slightly ticked-off but nonetheless thankful for the Freedom Account.

The following day being Saturday, Sam and Samantha decided to load the family in the car and head for the zoo. Halfway there and for absolutely no good reason, everything died—again! What is going on here? The Example family is miles from a service station and no one in this car has any mechanical ability.

However, this time they simultaneously exclaimed, "Aha!" and no one came even close to the panic stage. They had no choice but to call Al's Big Tow who charged $45 to haul them to Eddie's Electrical Shop. The kids thought it was pretty cool. Sam handed Al check #104 for $45, figured the balance to be $169.40 just in time to meet Eddie who quickly determined that the generator was shot and needed replacement. The bad news was $143.20. The good news was they had plenty to cover this maintenance item. Samantha wrote Eddie check #105 for $143.20, calculated the new balance of $26.20 and they were on their way to the zoo.

Let me explain what has just happened here. Sam and Samantha faced four auto repair situations within a three-day period. However, they were able to keep their cool, they paid in full for each item, and what would have normally been considered crises did not derail the Examples. They were able to handle each situation reasonably and appropriately. It was as if they were actually *prepared* for these kinds of inevitable repairs. In the future as they become more comfortable with their Freedom Account they will be able to head-off these kinds of repairs by practicing preventive maintenance. They will begin to assess tire wear, battery life, and generator performance before these parts are completely shot. By the way, by looking at the Example's Freedom Account, you will notice Sam had a major awakening in month 10. He figured that if he changed the oil himself, he could save money and afford to change it more often which is probably the single most important auto maintenance activity he could perform. He took advantage of a great sale and purchased twenty quarts of oil. He could no longer justify spending $29.95 to have it done when he could do it himself for less than $10 per change. In his pre–Freedom Account days the small difference between having it done and doing it himself didn't seem to make much difference. Things really have changed for the Examples.

How would Sam and Samantha have handled these situations a year ago, in their pre–Freedom Account days? First of all they would have seen each incident as a major crisis which resulted in stress, bad moods, yelling, and screaming. They would have bemoaned their bad luck and blamed the stupid car for preventing them from getting ahead. Because they wouldn't have had any more money in their Regular Account than they do now, they would've felt forced to do one of the following: break out the plastic and hope they had enough available credit to cover the emergency; call Mom and Dad for another bail-us-out loan; write a hot check and hope the merchant doesn't call to check before they can get the heck out of there; find some high-priced under-qualified auto repair joint that accepts their department store card. You laugh, but I think you're beginning to understand.

Start Slow and Easy

In the beginning I suggest that you set up your Freedom Account to handle the minimum number of *essential* Irregular Expenses. If you are too aggressive at first, the system will require a large monthly transfer and depending on your cash situation, you may be setting yourself up for failure. Start out simply and then gradually ease into expanding your Freedom Account.

Other Irregular Expenses

Some items are not as predictable as auto maintenance/repair and property taxes and have a way of hitting us over the head when we can least afford them.

For instance, an excellent way to keep insurance premiums low is to carry higher deductibles. But what happens if you are in an auto accident which requires you to fork over your $1,000 deductible? Ouch! That presents a huge problem for those who live paycheck to paycheck, spending every nickel and then some. I would advise adding a new sub-account to help with such potentially expensive emergencies.

Insurance Deductibles. This Freedom Account sub-account should grow until its balance is equal to the annual deductible of your health, homeowners and auto deductibles. If you are nervous about raising your deductibles in the beginning, go ahead and start a sub-account and when its balance reaches the amount equal to your current low deductibles, increase them so you will pay lower premiums. Imagine the peace of mind you will have knowing that the deductibles are there ready to be used if necessary, and if not, the account is drawing interest. That is freedom. Once your sub-account reaches the amount you determine is adequate to cover your deductibles, you as the manager of the account are free to divert future deposits into some other sub-account.

Clothing Account. You cannot imagine how many families do not list "clothing" when asked to list their expenses. But they don't walk around naked. Just the opposite, I have noticed that those in the worst financial shape are often the best-dressed. Where is that money supposed to come from? Many of course, load huge clothing expenses on credit cards or write checks using funds that were supposed to pay for groceries or utilities.

With a Freedom Account clothing becomes a dignified and legitimate monthly expense, while remaining affordable. You may want to set up a general Clothing Account for the entire family, or three separate accounts: His Clothes, Her Clothes, Kids' Clothes or some combination thereof.

Christmas/Holiday Account. Probably nothing in the world throws more of us into a debting depression faster than approaching the month of December. Broke! And every January you say that next year you are going to save a little bit every month for Christmas. And do you? Well, lest I sound like a broken record, your Freedom Account is the perfect way to set up your own Christmas Club.

Dream Accounts. What is it that you hope to have enough money to do or be someday? Perhaps you'd like to take a class, redecorate the master bedroom, go on a special trip, start a stamp collection, or take up skiing. If you are like most of us these things remain a dream to be fulfilled "when we get some extra money," which is never. Well, not anymore!

The Freedom Account is the way you are going to realize your dreams. Let your mind run wild. Insert new pages in your Freedom Account notebook and title them accordingly. Redecorate Master Bedroom, Room Addition, John's Woodworking Tools, Caribbean Cruise, Sam's Dream Account, Samantha's Dream Account, etc. Maybe you won't be able to start funding them right now, but little by little you are going to realize your dreams thanks to your Freedom Account.

I think the Freedom Account is a fabulous marriage tool. By having their individual accounts, both partners can manage some of their own money without feeling a need to sneak around or wallow in self-pity.

Unscheduled Income

This is any money which comes into your life irregularly or unpredictably such as rebate checks, tax refunds, freelance payments, gifts, etc. You receive unexpected and unpredictable money all the time. It may be only a dollar here or $10 there, but what happens to it? You put it in your pocket and it is absorbed into your daily spending so fast you hardly remember getting it. Larger amounts such as tax refunds and consulting payments usually go into the checking account with the intention they will be used in some special way, but before you know it—gone! And who knows where?

The Freedom Account is a wonderful solution to the case of the vanishing funds. Making a habit of depositing them—big or small—into the Freedom Account and selecting the sub-account to which they will be credited suddenly gives new meaning to surprise money. Let's say, for instance that you misjudged your Federal Tax Withholding and end up with a refund of $1,000. If you put it into your Regular Account it will be disappear, and eventually slip through your fingers via the ATM machine or some other phantom maneuver. But if you immediately put it into your Freedom Account you will be able to decide which dream to nourish.

COMMON QUESTIONS ABOUT A FREEDOM ACCOUNT

Q: Have you lost your mind? I don't have extra money every month to fund anything, let alone a Freedom Account.

A: Listen to yourself. You are acting as if maintaining your auto is optional or you can skip paying for your insurance if you're a little short. As if you have a choice whether or not to pay your property taxes or buy clothes? But you are driving a car, your taxes were paid, and you dress fairly well. Exactly how did you do that? You came up with the money somehow, and you probably have a few battle scars or credit card payments which help you remember the trouble you went through to do it.

This step is too important to pass off as something you cannot afford. I suggest you start out with the bare minimum number of accounts limiting them to your most essential Irregular Expenses. You may have to reduce your spending in other areas in order to get started with a Freedom Account, but whatever the sacrifice, no matter how painful, this is one of the nicest things you will ever do for yourself.

Q: Won't I incur new, unnecessary expenses caused by this new Freedom Account, expenses like fees for checks and service charges?

A: Yes. However, remember that as your total balance (the balance the bank sees is the total of all of your sub-accounts) grows beyond the minimum amount required, all service fees will be waived. You will be writing very few checks from this account so check costs will be minimal. I suggest that you choose your favorite account (in my case it would be "decorating" or "vacation") and designate it as the account from which you will deduct any "administrative" charges. However, this favorite account will also be credited all of the *interest* your Freedom Account will earn. If you are diligent in finding a bank that pays interest on checking accounts, you are going to make some good money which will be a great bonus for your favorite sub-account. Granted, the Freedom Account balance will fluctuate over the course of a year, but you are adding to it every month; this has a positive effect on your average daily balance. In time, you will earn a nice sum of reportable interest which should give your favorite account a mighty boost and more than offset any costs incurred.

Q: How do I balance the Freedom Account each month?

A: Add up the current balances of the sub-accounts. They should match the bank statement's closing balance once you have made allowances for checks which haven't cleared and deposits not yet posted. Balance it just like any other checking account. If you've never done this, step-by-step instructions can be found on the back of your monthly checking account statement. Now, in the event you are at all like me and break out in a rash at the very thought of mathematical calculations—don't panic. Some very kind employee in the new accounts department of your bank will be more than happy to teach you this surprisingly simple process.

Q: Couldn't I create my own Freedom Account at home without opening up another checking account?

A: Sure, you could get a series of envelopes and put cash into each one every month. But problems with this are obvious: Because keeping large sums of cash is not smart from a security standpoint you'd need a home safe or vault. Also it would be too easy to engage in impulsive borrowing. If things got a little rocky you might be tempted to skip a month or two. The Freedom Account should be a serious business activity, not a simple no-one-knows-if-I-do and no-one-knows-if-I-don't kind of thing. If you're at all like me, you need the discipline and pressure of an automatic withdrawal. It puts everything on a much higher, business-like, professional level. Besides, you probably won't pay yourself interest like the bank or credit union will. (I really like that interest!) Record-keeping is easier, too, when you have canceled checks at tax time.

Q: What happens if my Freedom Account gets too large? Shouldn't I be investing the money?

A: Remember this is not an investment vehicle, this is simply a money management tool. Most of your sub-accounts will be self-eliminating so you will never have continuously high balances. Sub-accounts such as insurance deductibles or other items which may not be self-eliminating, should have a cap. For instance, your insurance deductibles may total $1,000. Once you have reached the designated amount in your Deductibles sub-account, discontinue deposits until you must make a withdrawal. If you set up the Freedom Account properly, it is not going to present you with a problem of surpluses. Besides, I would hardly call that a problem. You will be amazed at how financially functional you'll become once you have the opportunity to manage your money.

Q: In the beginning as the sub-accounts have low balances, what will I do if I have an expense which is greater than the current balance in that sub-account?

A: Ideally you should find a way to open each sub-account with a larger initial deposit to cover this situation. Example: You open your Freedom Account on October 1. Your semiannual property tax bill is due on December 10. If your monthly property tax deposit into the Freedom Account is $75 you will hardly have the $450 necessary to make the payment. You will have contributed only $225 total ($75 × 3) into that particular sub-account. You should make an initial deposit into the sub-account to jump-start the process. By contributing an additional $225 into the account on October 1 to anticipate the shortfall, the problem would be solved. As you set up the Freedom Account you might see where a few hours of overtime or a moonlighting position for a few weeks would raise the funds necessary to launch your Freedom Account in such a way that you'll be fully prepared for the first expense. However, even if you can't manage the additional funding in the first month, don't let this become an excuse not to get started.

Let's look at another scenario. Say you have a $75 balance in your auto maintenance account and you incur a $150 repair item during the first month. What do you do? Write a check out of your Freedom Account for the $75 and supplement the balance from your Regular Account. Do NOT borrow from other freedom sub-accounts. While it pains me to suggest it, if you have absolutely no other way to come up with $75 (try hard—I mean REALLY hard). I feel it would be better this one last time to put the balance on a credit card and then pay the credit card payment from the auto maintenance sub-account. I would recommend this only if the borrowed funds can be repaid within the following 30 days. Example: Your auto maintenance/repair account has a balance of $75. Your repair bill is $150. You write a check for the $75 from the Freedom Account and pay for the balance on your credit card. By the time the billing comes you will have made another $75 deposit into the auto maintenance/repair sub account allowing you to write a check from the Freedom Account to pay off the credit card in full without incurring an interest charge. Going through these steps of depositing into the Freedom Account and writing a check out to cover the $75 credit card bill is necessary in order to keep everything straight and your sub-account page correct.

Accept the fact that it will take a little time to get the Freedom Account working smoothly. But don't let a little rough water in the beginning convince you to abandon such a wonderful, life changing tool!

. . . little did I know when I married my husband how important planning was to him. We sat down during our first year of marriage and established a goal of financial independence at age 55. "That's nice," I thought and went on with my teaching work.

Periodically, maybe once a year, we sat down again and estimated roughly the amount necessary to be taken out of our paycheck or bank account each month. The need for discipline was less because we never saw the money.

. . . I am happy to report we at age 50 are well on our way to our goal. Our savings is doing a great deal of work now. . . .

Muriel

CHAPTER 11

Rapid Debt-Repayment Plan: The Principle of Living Debt-Free

Like a lot of people I got my first credit card with a feeling of "having arrived" and declared it "only for emergencies." I still remember a coworker's laugh when I said that. Five years later I had six cards, all maxed out due to "emergencies" and then I understood what prompted her chuckle. I owe for car repairs on a car I no longer own; furniture that I sold in a garage sale; braces that came off my son's teeth a year ago but worst of all, my balances include several thousand dollars worth of expenses which I don't even remember.

Everyone who goes into debt and successfully digs out has a turning point. My turning point was arriving at Christmas time buried in bills with no space on any cards. I took a job working for minimum wage at a department store for the holidays. My entire Christmas season was miserable because I was so exhausted and had no time to enjoy festivities with my family. But it was such a valuable experience that I recommend this to anyone sinking into Credit Card Hell.

Working in that store, I saw credit from a whole different perspective. Customers would make a small payment on a huge balance, charge twice that while they were in the store and pay several times as much in the end on already overpriced merchandise because they had our credit line and no cash reserves. They bought top-of-the-line clothing and housewares to give as gifts in order to keep up appearances but confessed they would never be able to afford these things for themselves. As a cashier, I knew before they got to the register which customers would charge their purchase; they were the ones with the tired, sad expressions who were obviously not enjoying the holiday season or anything else. I felt guilty suggesting purchases (the training staff at this store instructed us to suggest the highest priced options and sell by pushing low payments, and never to divulge the number of payments) and putting their selections on account because I was helping make their lives worse. I even felt badly giving discounts to entice first time credit card buyers because I knew that the merchandise they were buying would not last as long as the payments. The giddy look on newlyweds' faces when they first discovered they had more buying power than cash looked sickeningly familiar.

That's the bad news.

The good news is for the first time in years I made up my mind to get off that merry-go-round forever. I am now going in the opposite direction—out of the hole instead of deeper in. Since the beginning of the year, I have devised and stuck with a two-year financial recovery plan and am beginning to see real results.

Ironically I am beginning to feel the same things I felt years ago when I got my first credit card: powerful, in charge, secure, and prepared for emergencies. Only this time, the emotions are based in reality.

Thank you again for your wonderful publications.

McKenzey

If you want to sabotage your Money Makeover *keep on incurring new debts!* That's right. Just keep those credit cards charged right up to the max, and as your income increases over the years make sure you get into as much debt as possible. This way no matter how much you work at reducing your expenses and saving for the future your debts will stick with you right to the grave, weighing you down and robbing you of happiness. You can make sure you are just one more who only dreamed of enjoying wonderful things and seeing beautiful places because you never quite got your money straightened out.

On the other hand, if you are excited about the possibilities of changing the way you deal with money, of developing new money attitudes, of experiencing happiness and satisfaction from knowing how to handle your resources in an intelligent and reasoned fashion, then it is mandatory you stop incurring debt and reverse the destructive behavior by making a Rapid Debt-Repayment Plan part of your Money Makeover.

Allow me to introduce you to a rarely thought of and even less enjoyable activity called *debt repayment*. This may come as a shock, but your debts have to be repaid somehow, somewhere, sometime. Hard as it is to believe, the credit card companies really are not in business to supply you with free clothes and fancy meals. That was a big shock to me too, but a terrible reality I had to face.

If you are relying on your minimum monthly payments to pay off your debt anytime soon, think again.

Let's say you owe $2,000 on your credit card which charges 19.8 percent interest for the privilege. Your minimum monthly payment is 4 percent of the outstanding balance, which is presently about $80 and fluctuates each month depending on the principle. Eighty dollars is all that's required so that's all you pay, right? Given the typical minimum payment requirements how long do you think it will take you to pay off that $2,000 even if you never make another purchase? Don't struggle too long with this math challenge. I'll tell you: 116 months. That's almost 10 years, assuming you are never late and do not add any new purchases. (Fat chance, huh?) By the time you're finished you will have paid interest in the amount of $1,215.44. And if you are a typical consumer, i.e., a preferred and valued customer, meaning you keep your credit cards "maxed out" or at least make sure there's a good, healthy balance rolling over from month to month, it is highly unlikely your consumer debt will ever be paid off. You will continue to pay this month for food you consumed years ago, clothes you've long since given away, and other stuff you've undoubtedly completely forgotten about. This, my friends, is known as perma-debt and the credit card companies love it.

Let's go back to that $2,000 debt example which has a current monthly minimum payment of $80. What if through some stroke of unexplained sense you made a solemn and personal pledge to pay $80 every month until the darned thing was paid in full, choosing to ignore the fact the actual monthly minimum payment requirement was going down every month? I'll tell you exactly what would happen: you would reach a zero balance in just 32 months, instead of 116. And if you got real sane and committed to pay $90 a month? The debt would be history in just 28 months. Brace yourself here, but let's assume you really lost your mind and made a personal pledge to pay $100 a month against this $2,000 debt. You would pay it off in just 24 months, more than *eight years sooner* than if you believed the credit card company when they said all you have to pay is the minimum monthly balance. I never cease to be amazed at the power of compounded interest and what it can do to one's financial picture!

All of us who are intimately familiar with over spending know that it is very easy to five-and-ten-dollar ourselves into oblivion. The good news is that you can five-and-ten-dollar yourself right back to financial health, too.

The key to rapid debt repayment is to make a plan and then stick to it as if your life depended on it. It may. The details of the plan you devise for your own debt reduction are not nearly as important as your determination to carry it out.

There are several methods of rapid debt reduction which work equally well. One method involves a plan whereby each of one's debts are paid off proportionately so that they all reach zero balance at the same time.

However, the method which I will teach you and which is, coincidentally, my personal favorite, is based on the principle that it feels good to work extra hard on one bill at a time in order to experience the exhilaration of a zero balance as quickly as possible. Paying off one debt completely gives a great boost to your determination to pay the next and the next and the next. While not instant gratification, this method certainly offers short-term achievable goals. Small dosages of gratification along the way keep one motivated. Here's how it works:

The first thing you must do is determine exactly how much you owe and the exact nature of your debts. We are talking about unsecured debt which includes credit card balances, personal loans, payments you are making to the dentist or doctor— anything that you owe but would not be subject to repossession if you stopped paying. Include all of your unsecured debts. Make a list which includes the current balance, minimum payment, interest rate and number of payments required to pay it in full. If you do not possess the math skills required to figure how many payments will be required to pay the debt off, you might consider using a financial calculator or just call the creditor and ask. With their super computer programs, they will be able to tell you. If you are a little confused, here is the question you should ask. "With my present balance of $_____, (insert your current balance) how many months will it take me to pay this debt in full if I make a monthly payment of $_____ (insert your present minimum monthly payment) every month and add no new purchases?"

Next arrange these debts in order of the number of months required to pay-in-full, with the shortest pay-off first on the list. (See Sam and Samantha Example's example which follows. The debt which they placed first on the list has a balance of $80. With a minimum payment of $35, it will take just a bit longer than two months to pay it off which is less than any of their other debts.) Next, add up the total of the current minimum monthly payments.

This is a very important number so write it down, embed it in your brain, tattoo it on your forehead, paint it on your walls, teach it to your children. Forgive me, I go a little nuts now and again. You can skip the tattoo.

And now . . . it's commitment time. Look again at the total of your minimum monthly payments, that number you've just embedded in your brain. This is the amount of money you must commit to pay toward your Rapid Debt-Repayment Plan until all of your debts are paid. I don't think you should find this at all out of line, because this is the amount you have to pay every month whether you ever picked up this book or not. At this time I am not asking you to pay any more than you are required to pay. (It wouldn't be such a bad idea, but it's not required.) This is the minimum amount you must devote to your rapid debt repayment plan regardless if the minimum amount the creditor says you owe in one particular month goes down or not. Remember they want you to pay less every month so you can keep paying forever.

Look at The Example's Rapid Debt-Repayment Plan which follows. Basically this is how it works. The total of the minimum monthly payments in the first month is $619. This is the amount our Example Family has committed to pay every month until they are debt-free, regardless of anything their creditors say about lower payments. In Month 1, the Examples make all of the minimum monthly payments for a total of $619. In Month 2 they do the very same thing. In Month 3, they make their committed payments just like in the past two months—except, the payment to the Department Store #1 is only $12 because that is the total outstanding balance. Wow! The first zero balance. So what happens to the $23 they didn't have to send to Department Store #1 because of the zero balance? Should they use it to celebrate the first victory? No! That $23 must be included with the regular payment to Personal Loan (the next debt in line), increasing its payment from $108 to $131.

In Month 4 the $35 payment which used to go to

Department Store #1 is now added to Personal Loan's payment so it becomes $143. This additional payment (technically prepayment of the principle) is what will get that Personal Loan paid in just seven months, including interest. The total amount paid in Month 4 is still $619 even though the number of debts has been reduced.

Now look at what happened to the Student Loan while this was going on. It reached a zero balance in Month 4 as well, so now Sam and Samantha have three debts completely paid off. But since they are committed to paying $619 every month against their debts, the payment to Visa #1 is substantially increased because the old payments for Department Store #1, Personal Loan, and Student Loan are all added to the Visa #1 payment increasing it from $108 to $277 until it is fully paid in Month 11.

And on it goes. The Examples pay $619 every month, always taking the old payments and adding them to the payment of the next debt in line until they are 100 percent debt-free in Month 23! You must agree that this is truly amazing, considering that given the slow-pay method, Sam and Samantha would have been paying on these debts for 12 or more years, provided of course that they never missed a payment and did not incur any new debt.

Summary: Here are the five steps for wiping out your debts in record time:

Rapid Debt-Repayment Plan

Sam and Samantha Example

(Debt-Free in just 24 months! 🏃)

Creditor	$ Bal	%	1	2	3	4	5	6	7	8	9	10	11	12	13	14	15	16	17	18	19	20	21	22	23	24	25	26	27
Dept. Store # 1	180	16.9%	36	86	112	0																							
Personal Loan	700	10%	106	108	131	143	69	0																					
Student Loan	200	6%	26	26	26	26	28	74	0																				
Visa # 1	1,500	10%	108	108	108	108	114	277	277	277	277	277	209	0															
Orthodontist	1,000	10%	40	40	40	40	40	40	40	40	40	40	106	306	369	0													
Credit Union	3,000	12%	120	120	120	120	120	120	120	120	120	120	120	120	136	437	437	437	437	437	145	0							
Finance Co.	1,200	14%	45	45	45	45	45	45	45	45	45	45	45	45	45	45	45	45	45	45	337	276	0						
MasterCard	1,000	19.6%	40	40	40	40	40	40	40	40	40	40	40	40	40	40	40	40	40	40	40	244	204	0					
Visa # 2	650	10%	32	32	32	32	32	32	32	32	32	32	32	32	32	32	32	32	32	32	32	32	125	0					
Dept. Store # 2	2,000	10.5%	66	66	66	66	66	66	66	66	66	66	66	66	66	66	66	66	66	66	66	66	227	619	519	0			
Totals	$11,330		619	619	619	619	619	619	619	619	619	619	619	619	619	619	619	619	619	619	619	619	619	619	519	DEBT-FREE!!			

Fig. 11-1

1. You must repent. "Repent" simply means to turn around, to go in a different direction. You must repent from "debting," that is, incurring new debts. If you don't complete the first step the plan will not work.

2. You must pay the same amount every month until all of your unsecured debts are paid in full. From this moment on you must adopt the total of your current minimum monthly payments as your regular monthly obligation, not unlike your house or car payment. It will not change from month to month. It's big, it's ugly, and it's not going away. Just accept it.

3. List your debts in order according to the number of months left. For example, a debt to a department store of $80 total with a minimum monthly payment of $40 has about two months left (the total paid will be slightly higher than the $80 because of the interest). That one goes at the top of your list.

4. From here on out ignore declining minimum monthly payments. Whatever the minimum is in the first month is the amount you are going to pay until your total debt is wiped out, regardless of whether the creditor shows a lower amount due on your statement.

5. As one debt is paid off apply its monthly payment to the next debt. No matter how many debts you have paid off, you must commit to pay the same total amount every month until every debt is paid.

If you want to see your Rapid Debt-Repayment Plan work even more quickly, increase your monthly commitment. Remember that the key to rapid repayment is in prepaying principle.

. . . with your help I have comprised a debt repayment plan. I will be debt-free on New Year's Eve! Don't you agree that is the best way to start the new year? I sure do.

Being debt-free will allow me to finally quit a job I hate and attend college full-time. Every day I become more motivated as the day comes closer.

Richele

Just want to say thank you—you've really opened my eyes. My Rapid Debt-Repayment Plan has me completely paid off in 36 months.

I was $14,000 in credit card debt. You're right, you get into a set pace of living the good life without realizing what you are doing to your future. In one month I charged $1,428 in clothing on my Visa card without a second thought. (At 21 percent interest!)

I'm on the road to recovery. I got into the habit of living well when I married a man who made an incredible salary; when we divorced it was nearly impossible to cut back. I tried to maintain the lifestyle to which I'd become accustomed. I've had to face reality and it's been tough.

I'll be completely debt-free when I'm 34 years old and I can't wait!

Mary Beth

. . . I wanted to let you know how we are "digging out!" We were able to refinance our home which not only reduced the payment, but yielded some cash which we used to pay off several high interest credit cards. Our credit card–cutting ceremony took quite a while because we had so many. What a relief that was! My husband was not as eager as I to take such a drastic measure and it took a lot of convincing but he finally agreed. With the money that was freed up because of the lower mortgage payment we have made substantial monthly payments on a couple of remaining cards (we had 28 total). . . . It will take about six more months to pay them off in full.

I am projecting by March we will pay the last outstanding debt and be debt-free, with the exception of our huge mortgage. But with no other payments we will pay it off in 15 years using a method you recommended in a recent issue of *Cheapskate Monthly*.

Thank you so much for your encouragement . . . you've made our lives much easier to bear and we'll always be grateful!

Nancy

CHAPTER 12

Monthly Spending Plan:
The Principle of Restraint

"Thanks for your book—I believe your plan has saved me from a life of debt. Thanks too for showing me that a financial plan doesn't have to be scary or use complicated mathematics."

Tracy

It's time to start drawing your monthly financial blueprint. Don't leave me now! And don't panic. This is not a budget and you are not about to slip into a straitjacket. I am going to help you get your finances down on paper so that you will know exactly how to take the first step, the second step, the third step . . . and the 96th step if necessary in reaching the goal of living joyfully beneath your means. Learning to live with a Monthly Spending Plan is the best way I know of to experience financial peace of mind.

So far we have determined that the key to balancing your finances is to start saving, start giving, prepare for irregular expenses with a Freedom Account, and stop the debt spiral by repaying debts quickly. Now we need to take control of the day-by-day spending that seems so out of whack.

You will need a few tools in order to get started: a pencil, pad of paper, and calculator. If you want to get really fancy you can pick up a ledger or budget book at your office supply store or dust off that financial software or spreadsheet program you bought for your personal computer. Any of these things will work just fine to assist in drawing up this "blueprint."

Step 1. Determine your Average Monthly Income. Regardless of your payroll schedule or the frequency with which you receive other sources of income, you must come up with your average monthly income, that number which when multiplied by twelve equals your annual gross income. You will be working with gross, that is, before tax, figures.

NOTE: If you are self-employed as an entrepreneur or commissioned salesperson, don't think this chapter cannot apply to you. However, you may wish to jump ahead to Chapter 14 to learn how to determine your Average Monthly Income before going farther in this chapter.

When coming up with this income figure, include all sources of income such as salary, wages, dividend and interest income, child support payments, alimony, etc., using *before tax figures.* If you get this money on a regular basis, can predict its arrival, and can spend it, it's income.

Here's a quick formula to determine your average monthly income if you receive it other than once a month:

Weekly:	Multiply your weekly income by 4.333
Biweekly:	Multiply your biweekly income by 2.167
Semi-monthly:	Multiply your semi-monthly income by 2
Quarterly:	Divide your quarterly income by 3
Annually:	Divide your annual income by 12

Why should you use pretax income figures? Because everything withheld from your taxes represents "expenses" that you are obligated to pay even though some of those deductions may well be savings or retirement plans. These are expenses just like your rent and food and it is important that you begin to recognize them as such. Your health insurance premiums and all of those other amounts which keep showing up as deductions on your pay stub are expenses that you pay. Some of those deductions may be optional, meaning you have the ability to eliminate or change them.

Back to your income. Once you have come up with your accurate average monthly income figure, write that number down. We'll be using it later.

Step 2. Make a list of your Expense Categories.
You have fixed expenses (car payment, rent, mortgage payment, etc.) and flexible expenses (food,
gasoline, telephone, utilities, etc.) Refer to the Possible Expense Categories List at the end of this chapter to help you remember all of the ways that you
spend money. This is an exhaustive list of every type
of expense I could think of divided into main categories and sub-categories. Just pick out the ones
which apply to you. You might want to use the main
categories such as Housing, Transportation, etc., or
you might want to go into more detail. You can com-
bine categories or add new ones. The point is that
your list of Expense Categories should be unique to
you and your family. *Do not repeat any of the categories
which have already been listed in your Freedom Account
Notebook or Rapid Debt-Repayment Plan.* Instead, list
"Freedom Account" as one category and "Rapid
Debt-Repayment Plan" as another. Be sure to include categories for Saving and Giving.

Try to be neither too detailed nor too general.
Too many categories will be unmanageable. Too few
categories will give you only a vague idea of where
you are. I recommend the average family should
have 10–20 categories on their Monthly Spending
Plan, including the four mandatory categories of
Savings, Giving, Freedom Account, and Rapid Debt-
Repayment Plan. Don't forget to include categories
for Federal and State tax withholding, social security, and other payroll deductions. These are major
expenses which we often fail to take into consider-

ation when looking at our total financial picture. I suggest you have one category for Taxes (State, Federal, and Social Security, which is also referred to as FICA) and then another category, "Other Withholding," to handle everything else.

To make sure you haven't forgotten anything, take a quick jaunt through your checkbook register, your payroll stubs and your paid bills folder to see how you spent your money in the last two or three months. Take note of your ATM withdrawals. (Have any idea where that money went?) This whole exercise should help you come up with an idea of your typical monthly expenses.

Step 3. Draft Your Monthly Spending Plan. Get a sheet of paper and make up a form using Figure 12-1 as your guide. Transfer your Expense Categories to the Monthly Spending Plan form. Using the past as an indicator, fill in the "Plan" column across from each category with the dollar amount you plan to spend in each category during the next month. The "E/O" column is where you will honestly indicate whether this expense is "essential" or "optional." Make sure you have not combined any essential expenses with optional ones when you made up your category list. You may need to do some real soul-searching when you make this determination for each entry. For example, I know you probably prefer to think of cable TV or your cellular phone as essential expenses. They aren't, trust me. Mark them "O."

Monthly Spending Plan
Month of August, 1994

Category	WK 1	WK 2	WK 3	WK 4	Actual $ Spent in Mo.	Plan $ to Spend in Mo.	Amt. $ +/-	E/O
Savings	100		100		200	200	—	E
Giving	100		100		200	200	—	E
Freedom Account	320				320	320	—	E
Rapid Debt Repayment Plan	619				619	619	—	E
Mortgage Payment			850		850	850	—	E
Car Payment		172			172	172	—	E
Gasoline	18	21	16	15	70	80	- 10	E
Groceries	70	72	78	65	285	300	- 15	E
Food & Out	35	27	14	40	116	75	+ 41	O
Utilities			155		155	180	- 25	E
Telephone				24	24	37	- 13	E
Fed & State Taxes	816				816	816	—	E
Other Withholding	256				256	256	—	E
Babysitter	10			10	20	25	-5	O
Kids' Allowances		20			20	20	—	O
Newspapers/magazines	3	5	6	2	16	20	- 4	O
Totals	2347	317	1319	156	4139	4170	-31	

Average Monthly Income: $ ___$4,583.00___

Total Actual $ Spent this month: $ — 4,139.00___

Underspent or <Overspent> $ __444.00___

If overspent $_____ ÷ Income $_____ = _____% reduction required for next month

Fig. 12-1

When you have completed filling in an amount for each category, calculate and enter the total of your planned spending. Now fill in your average monthly income. Take a deep breath, go get a glass of water, and compare those two figures ("Plan" column total and Average Monthly Income).

If your planned spending is more than your income perhaps we have begun to uncover the root of your financial problems. If your "Plan" column came in less than your income, go on to the next step. If not, now is the time to decide what you are going to do about this situation. You cannot go on spending more money than you have each month.

Since you have determined to stop relying on credit to cover your regular expenses, and allowing your bills to become delinquent is no longer an option, you must find ways to reduce your regular monthly expenses.

Go back over each category, one by one. You may need to eliminate some of your "optional" entries for a while. Small sacrifices will reward you well in the future. You know you cannot mess with the Freedom Account (unless, of course, you have included sub-accounts which represent optional spending and could be eliminated for the time being) or your Rapid Debt-Repayment Plan. Your new commitment to these areas of planning ahead and paying off debt are absolutely essential to your makeover.

You will probably need to redraw this initial Monthly Spending Plan many times until you get it just right.

Sometime before the first day of the month for which you have designed this Monthly Spending Plan you should have things organized. Let me assure you that your plan will be in a constant state of change, so don't feel defeated if you don't get it exactly right in the first few months.

Step 4: How to Activate Your Monthly Spending Plan. It's nice to have a great-looking Monthly Spending Plan, but unless you activate it, it's not going to do you much good.

From now on you will look at each month as having four weeks regardless of what day of the week the first falls on or how many total days are in the month: Days 1–7 will always be Week 1; Days 8–14 will always be Week 2; Days 15–21, Week 3; Days 22– End of Month, Week 4. It doesn't matter that the fourth week of every month will have anywhere from six to nine days.

Step 5: Counting and Recording. One of your new mandatory behaviors has to do with counting and recording. As the month begins it is necessary that you and anyone else who spends the family's income agrees to keep a written notation of how the money was spent. Not difficult, but extremely necessary. Every expenditure, no matter how small, must be accounted for and recorded from now on. Here's how you will do it. As you spend during the week, write down two things: What for? and How much? Every time you spend cash or write a check, you must record it. At the end of each week, tally up all expenditures for the week and record these totals by category in the appropriate "week" column on your Monthly Spending Plan. You may find yourself reworking your categories when you can't figure out which category to put "Newspaper—35¢" in, for example.

Step 6: Month-End Truth. On the last day of the month (which will always be the last day of Week 4) fill in the last column, "Wk 4," with your expenses from Week 4. Run individual category totals across and enter the amounts in the "Actual" column. Did you go over or under your "Plan" amount in each category? Enter the difference in the "+/−" column.

Now total the "Actual" column adding up what you actually spent in all categories. How does this compare up with your "Plan" column?

Let me predict what happened during this first month: 1. You had expenditures for which you had prepared no categories. 2. You spent far more than you had planned and found yourself hopelessly broke and dying to write a bad check in Week 4. *Failure to acknowledge your true expenses is the reason you have lost control of your finances.* You didn't mean to overspend—you were simply unaware of your true expenses! Hopefully you have a lot more insight now than you had a month ago.

Here's the beautiful thing about a Monthly Spending Plan: You are in charge! As a good manager, you need to start planning immediately for next month.

Step 7: Rethink Optionals: A logical place to cut expenses is in the area of nonessential items. Perhaps canceling cable TV or mowing the yard yourself might be in order for a while in order to reduce expenses. Maybe you've been indulging in luxuries that you really cannot afford at this time.

Step 8: Prepare next months' Spending Plan. This is going to be easy because you have all the figures from last month. As you fill in the "Plan" column, use the data from last months' "Actual" column to give you a starting point. Look at your flexible categories such as food or utilities. How much could you reasonably reduce those items in the coming month? How much do you need to reduce spending in this area next month in order to come in under plan? Plug in a figure and then do everything you can to reach the goal.

A Monthly Spending Plan is absolutely mandatory if you want to achieve financial independence. It doesn't take time, it saves time. It doesn't prevent you from having the desires of your heart, it takes you from dreams to reality.

Living with a Monthly Spending Plan

From now on you will have two basic financial tools—your checkbook and your Monthly Spending Plan. This is where it gets a little tricky, but as long as you understand the function of each you should not have a problem.

Basically, you must live according to your Monthly Spending Plan. For instance, perhaps you have designated $200 as your planned spending in the category of "Groceries" for the month. You need to spend no more than $200 just as the plan states. However, your cash flow may ebb and flow through the month and if you have a current balance of $4.32 in your Regular Account, you'd best not run out and purchase $200 in groceries simply because that is the amount you have allotted on your Monthly Spending Plan!

You have based your Monthly Spending Plan on your *average monthly income*. Because your paycheck and other sources of income may not arrive on time, you may need to adjust and fine-tune the timing of your spending to accommodate your "cash flow." There will be times when you need to delay expenditures so that you do not move ahead of your deposits.

On the other hand, there will be months when your actual income is significantly greater than your monthly planned spending. This is where you will need all of the discipline and restraint you can muster. Your common sense will tell you that the balance in the checkbook is not some newfound windfall. While I know that a balance of any significance in your Regular Checking account may not be something you're familiar with, get familiar with it. If you work your makeover right, this will happen, so keep your grubby hands off of it! Your *average* monthly income has not changed; don't live as though it has.

You remember figuring "averages" in math class, don't you? You added up a list of numbers; some were small, others were large, but when you added them up and divided by the total number of entries in your list you ended up with the average.

The same principle is true of your income. Some months your actual income will be one of the smaller numbers in the list, other months it will be a larger one. But if you spend up the excess or the amount over the average because you see a balance in the checking account, you are going to be in big trouble next month, or the next. For example, let's suppose you make $36,000 a year, paid every other week. Your average monthly income is $3,000, but ten months a year you will get two paychecks totally $2,769.23 and two months a year you'll get three checks totaling $4,153.85.

Perhaps it's time for you to force a little financial maturity upon yourself. It's okay to have a balance in your checking account. It will not burn a hole there, just keep your mitts off it and allow your Money Makeover plan to work. Believe me, it will all come out right by the end of the year if you will be patient, diligent, persistent, mature and disciplined.

I encourage you to take the simple Monthly Spending Plan and expand or enhance it so that your makeover becomes uniquely yours. I don't know what will work for you on a day-to-day basis. Perhaps you will want to use envelopes or coffee cans to keep your spending straight. I don't want to tell you how often to go to the grocery store. I do know what works for me, but it may not work for you. (We grocery shop once a month, buy in bulk—and make it last. There have been times we've shopped for two months which presents a whole new twist when living by a Monthly Spending Plan.)

Optimize your growth by consciously focusing on restraint. It is the lack of restraint that has caused you to make some foolish purchases in the past for which you may still be paying. Restraint is good, because it allows you to bring into action all of your intelligence and reason which you often ignored when you lived impulsively and made off-the-cuff financial decisions.

You possess more power that you could ever imagine. I want to challenge you to harness that power, just like a dam harnesses the power of a raging river and uses that power to produce electricity. There is no limit to what you can accomplish once you harness your strength, your abilities, your talents, and your determination!

On the following page you will find a hypothetical Monthly Spending Plan for our friends, Sam and

Samantha Example. Remember, this is hypothetical and in no way suggests a perfect scenario. Use it as an example for creating your own plan.

You will notice that the Examples' savings and giving amount to about 5 percent of their gross income. While not optimum, this is certainly a healthy start. Please keep in mind that the giving category reflects only cash contributions and does not reflect nonmonetary gifts of time or talent.

You may be curious as to why the Examples have so few categories on their plan. This is the beautiful thing about having a Freedom Account and a Rapid Debt-Repayment Plan. None of the categories covered there needs to be repeated. The simple entries "Freedom Account" and "Rapid Debt-Repayment Plan" take care of it. Categories such as clothing, entertainment, medical/dental, etc. would not show up individually on the Monthly Spending Plan, but would be handled in the Freedom Account.

You will notice that the Examples underspent by $391 in the month of August 1994. They are living beneath their means! I would recommend that they leave this balance in their Regular Checking Account as a cushion. Eventually, if this excess continues on a regular basis I would recommend they increase their savings allotment and devote the rest to their Rapid Debt-Repayment amount.

Two years from now when they have completed their Rapid Debt-Repayment Plan, the Examples will immediately have $619 "extra" each month. What should they do? Wow! Their choices are many.

They could open a New Car sub-account in their Freedom Account and fund it to the tune of $619 each month; they could split that amount between several existing Freedom Account sub-accounts; or they could start prepaying their mortgage by that amount each month. They could expect to pay off their home mortgage in record time with that kind of healthy prepayment of principle.

Options. The wise management of our money gives us wonderful options and that's what a Money Makeover is all about!

List of Possible Expenses

Giving
Church/Synagogue
Charities

Savings
Investment
College
Other
Retirement

Freedom Account

Rapid-Debt-Repayment Plan

Housing
Mortgage payment
Rent

Utilities
Electricity
Water
Gas
Heating oil
Telephone
Cable TV
Trash pick-up

Home maintenance
Maintenance
Grounds care
Other

Food
Groceries
Business lunches
Fast food
Restaurants
School lunches
Other

Clothing
Adult
Children
Laundry
Dry cleaning
Other

Medical
Medicine/Drugs
Dental
Eyeglasses

Doctor and dentist visits
Medical insurance
Dental insurance
Hospital costs
Other

Transportation
Licensing/Registration
Gasoline
Oil/Antifreeze
Tires
Repairs
Inspection
Parking
Public transportation
Other

Gift
Birthdays
Anniversaries
Business-related
Wedding/Baby
Christmas/Holiday
Other

Recreation/Entertainment
Vacations
Shows/Movies
Sporting events
Dining
Clubs
Parties

Hobbies
Other

Personal/Household
Furniture
Kitchen appliances
Utility appliances
Electronic appliances
Linens
Utensils
Tools
Beauty shop and supplies
Barber shop and supplies
Fitness center
Toiletries
Reading material
Pets and supplies
Veterinarian

Insurance
Auto
Life
Property/Casualty
Renter
Other

Taxes (Withheld)
Income (Federal)
State (Federal)
Social Security (FICA)
Other

Other Payroll Withholding
Health insurance
Disability
Unemployment insurance

Support/Child Care
Alimony
Child support
Day care
Baby-sitting
Support of parents
Children's allowances
Other

Miscellaneous
Tuition
School supplies
School room and board
Athletic fees
Union dues
Professional fees
Licenses
Lessons
Other

CHAPTER 13

How To Live Within Your Means

If your efforts to design a Monthly Spending Plan that fits within your income have left you with a three-alarm headache and a feeling of defeat, take heart. You are not alone and there are remedies. If you are determined, nothing can stop you. But there are no instant solutions, this process takes time. You must never give up. In time you will be able to look back in amazement to see that by taking one step at a time you were able to completely change the direction of your life. Don't ever underestimate the power of the simplest step you take to bring your income and your spending in line. Remember, if you don't change the direction you're going in, you will end up where you're headed.

There are only three ways you can change the numbers on your Monthly Spending Plan.

1. Increase your income.
2. Sell your assets.
3. Decrease your expenses.

Increasing Income. This is probably the first thing most of us consider when facing financial hardship because it appears to be the quickest and most painless solution. However, of the three remedies listed above, I believe this is the least desirable. Increasing income does nothing to address the root problem of habitual overspending. More money just provides more opportunity and greater ability to overspend, and allows the debt-prone individual to qualify for more debt. Increasing income invariably increases expenses in the form of taxes, child care, transportation, clothing, and meals out. It takes a great deal of additional income to realize a substantial net effect after all the tax collectors have taken their share.

Think about the effect that increasing your income has had in the past. Think back five years. You have increased your income since then, so why wasn't that the solution?

Selling assets. This is an excellent way to make a one-time or occasional positive adjustment in your Monthly Spending Plan provided you have assets with a resale value. The best way to find out if you do is to make a list of everything you own. Take each item and assign to it a market value, the amount you could reasonably sell it for within the next 90 days. (This is not a bad exercise to go through once a year, even if you have no intention of selling anything.)

Next, go through your list and rate each item according to this criteria:

Things I don't want to keep
Things I could live without
Things I can't live without

You might be amazed at the total market value of all the stuff cluttering up your home and your life that you could easily live without. Every day people just like you are getting extra cash by selling things they no longer use or need. I suggest you cautiously decide what you have that you can actually live without. Don't make hasty decisions or you may live to regret selling something that you still need.

Holding a garage sale is an excellent way to liquidate low-priced goods. For more valuable things, consult with an antique dealer or consignment store owner. Perhaps your area has an auction which accepts items along the lines of those you wish to sell. Look through your local classified ads to see what price others are asking for similar items. Study the ads to see which ones are the most appealing. Practice writing your own compelling ad. Let your friends and neighbors know of anything you have for sale. Your best customer might be right under your nose.

Money realized from selling assets can be used in several ways: To speed up the Rapid Debt-Repayment Plan; to increase the monthly income in the month in which the transaction takes place; to deposit the funds in one or more sub-accounts of your Freedom Account thereby reducing the monthly withdrawal from your Regular Account.

Selling assets is a good way to raise your income but not many of us can count on hosting a successful garage sale more than once a year or so. However, by using the proceeds to pay down debt the net effect on your bottom line will be permanent. If you apply the proceeds to meet your regular monthly expenses the result will have an effect only in that month.

Decreasing expenses. Cutting expenses is by far the most desirable way to increase income. Example: If you work overtime in order to earn an additional $100 you will be lucky to see $50 which you can be applied to your Monthly Spending Plan. However, if you cut $100 from your monthly food bill, you will instantly see a $100 net effect on your Monthly Spending Plan's bottom line month after month.

Decreasing expenses has many other benefits which make this by far the quickest and best way to get your income and your expenses in line. By forcing you to pay attention to what you are spending and finding ways to spend less you'll increase your consciousness about spending, you'll become a better steward of what you have, and you will be better able to see which things in life really matter. You'll reclaim your home as you gradually de-junk your life. You'll become more appreciative by waiting until you can purchase something with Cash! You will find flexibility in living as you shed heavy debilitating debt. You'll find yourself more flexible, and you'll travel through life with a spring in your step rather than a pain in your neck!

The idea of reducing your living expenses to eighty percent of your income might seem ridiculously impossible right now. But it's not. We humans are amazing creatures. How few our true needs, how vast our wants! The trick to achieving this incredible reducing act is in assessing our present situation, deciding what percentage of reduction must take place and then proceeding to work on every area accordingly. It can be done. You have a new mission in life: save money any way you can!

There are literally thousands of ways to cut your expenses. However, until you have a plan and a way to measure the effect of cutting expenses it seems quite meaningless to save a dollar here when we are in a major financial crunch. To be quite honest it seems as frustrating as trying to drain the ocean cup by cup. It is this kind of frustration which often prevents us from making any change in our spending habits. But when you have a clear-cut Monthly Spending Plan in mind these savings multiplied over and over will be the very thing that makes the unbelievable possible.

Tricks of the Trade

Because you are going to become increasingly conscious of every penny you spend (you will be writing it down), you can train yourself to approach spending in a new way. From now on, before you make a significant purchase (you decide what significant is, perhaps anything over $20?), stop for a second and ask these questions:

Do I really need this? If the answer is "yes" go on. If the answer is "no," bravo! You just saved yourself from a stupid purchase.

Do I already have something that would do just as well? If the answer is "yes," you've just saved yourself from an unwise purchase. If the answer is "no," go on.

Could I find a cheaper substitute? If the answer is "yes," don't buy now. If the answer is "no," go on.

If after applying this little test you find you need it, you don't have anything else that would do just as well, and you need all the quality you can afford, go ahead and make your selection. And then? WAIT, for a full 24 hours—a full week is far more desirable —until you actually make the purchase. End result? If you really go through with the transaction, and you won't believe how many times you'll change your mind during the mandatory waiting period, you never will wonder if it was the right thing to do.

As much as possible, live with CASH

When I refer to "CASH," I mean full payment up front—no credit cards, no bad checks, no games, no manipulation.

For a long time the only way I could guarantee that kind of honest transaction was to pay for everything with cash. I was too crazy with a checkbook, and credit cards were out of the question. I have, however, become quite responsible with a business checking account over the past few years and can even be trusted with our personal checkbook. I haven't bounced a check in nearly twelve years! In some ways I have become obsessive about not messing up by balancing on a daily basis. It works for me so that's what I do. But for day-to-day, non-business purchases, I use CASH. I haven't been mugged and don't even worry about it because I carry so little cash at any one time.

I recommend that anyone with an overspending problem chuck the checkbook and credit cards and depend on cash and/or money orders. This will put the brakes on the insanity of spending money you don't have. And my experience is that if you force yourself to live with CASH you will spend less because this forces you to be a much more careful consumer. Try it the next time you go to the grocery store. Leave the checkbook at home and take just the amount of money you have allotted for groceries.

Never buy better quality than you need. For example, if you need something for a single use, you might be wise to buy the cheapest thing you can find, or rent it. But when it comes to something like a mattress, which you want to last for many years and consistently give you a great night's rest, you would be well-advised to buy the highest quality you can possibly afford to buy with CASH.

Never buy new until you have considered used. The secondary market in this country for everything from automobiles to zithers is absolutely astounding. I'm not saying you should never buy anything new again, just consider used before possibly paying five to 10 times as much for new. You're going to love what that kind of transaction does for your Monthly Spending Plan!

The wonderful thing about living within your means is that as you practice saving and giving, as you assess your true needs and put your wants and desires into proper perspective, and as you plan for the future, your anxiety level diminishes and abundance begins to flow—abundance in the form of contentment and joy as well as money and material things. The balance is rewarded. I can't explain it, I just accept it. Joyfully!

As your means change

Now is the time to determine how you will handle additional future income or decreases in present income. Don't be so naive as to think your average monthly income will never change.

Failure to plan for such occurrences is what happened to you in the past. As your income increased, you hardly noticed it because of all the overspending you were doing. When it decreased, the bottom fell out of your world.

Using Sam and Samantha as an example, let's say that Sam receives a ten percent salary increase on January 1. If they have not planned ahead for such an occurrence it is very likely the Examples could head into the new year with a false sense of having $5,000 extra to SPEND! And what about the new income Samantha will be generating from her home-based desktop publishing business? Without the security of knowing exactly how to handle these increases in their income, they could very easily be deceived to believe they can go out and buy all kinds of neat stuff. On the other hand, what if Sam gets laid off and has a ninety-day period of unemployment?

I know this is going to sound like a tired old broken record, but you must start with step one and go right on through. And Step One was? Determine your Average Monthly Income. So back to the plan board you go, adjusting figures so that you come up with your new Average Monthly Income.

Next you must go to your Monthly Spending Plan and start adjusting. Savings need to be increased or decreased to reflect the new income base. Giving must be adjusted. Taxes, and other withholding must be adjusted to account for the increased income or lack thereof.

Once these adjustments are made, I would recommend that you leave your spending plan alone for the time being if the adjustment is caused by an increase in income. Give your new situation three or four months to settle in. If you see that you are consistently spending well under your income, readjust.

Perhaps now would be the time to increase your entertainment allotment, increase your deposits, or add new sub-accounts to the Freedom Account or boost your Rapid Debt-Repayment monthly allotment. The key is that as your income increases, you respond cautiously and slowly. Don't blow it by jumping into same outrageous new debt.

Eventually, as an experienced financial manager, you will know when you're ready to take on a larger mortgage or higher rent. You'll know when it's the right time to buy another car (with CASH) or take the cruise you've been dreaming about.

And if the adjustment is due to a decrease in income? Then you need to go right down the list and adjust those figures according to the percentage drop in income. It could be a bleak picture, or if you have been diligent in paying off debt—you might be pleasantly surprised how flexible you have become.

The key is in finding balance and planning ahead. Determine ahead of time exactly how and what you will adjust if and when your income changes. It may well·go up, and then on the other hand, it could go down! The steps in adjusting your Monthly Spending Plan will remain the same.

. . . I recently decided to do something about weight-control, but as a fellow cheapskate I was determined not to spend a fortune on diet drinks, nutrition bars, and diet entrees. I had been trying since last year to get our weekly food bill down to $50. I had not been able to achieve it even though I was keeping track of every penny I spent for food. Including meals out I was averaging $83 per week for a family of four so I was determined not to let this diet make my food spending go up.

I changed some of my buying habits. I bought more fruit, whole grain cereal, tuna, and celery and fewer prepackaged sweets. Since I was trying to cut down on fats, I bought less meat and more potatoes and rice.

To date the family total weight loss is twenty-one pounds, but the incredible part of this letter—my food spending is hovering right at $50 a week! So we are spending less, a lot less—actually $138 less and we are all eating healthier!

Betty

. . . we paid off all of "my" debts in March. We replaced our water heater, fixed my double oven and bought a convection oven—all with CASH! We're getting ready to tile our floors and do some major renovations—all with CASH!

In four years our car will be paid off and so will our mortgage. At that time I will be fifty-one and it's great knowing we have things under control. Only wish I'd wised up years ago. With discipline anyone can do what we have. My advice is don't give up.

Molly

CHAPTER 14

Raising Financially Responsible Children

I cannot think of a profession more challenging or more noble than parenthood. It's not like a challenging career or rough course of study that can be abandoned should it turn out to be beyond our capability or if we simply change our minds. But the greater the challenge, the greater the reward, and in no situation is this more true than in raising financially responsible children.

The key to successful parenting lies in our ability to pass the baton of our faith and our values, including our financial values, along to our children.

The passing process must be deliberate and well thought-out. First and most important, the parent must have a clear-cut set of values, something worth passing on! Next, this "baton" must be passed at the appropriate time, on an appropriate level, and at the right speed. Lastly, the child must be in a position with hand outstretched and heart opened in order to receive it and carry it on to the next generation.

Unlike a relay race where the participants have only a split second to accomplish a flawless transfer, parents have a considerably longer period of time in which to develop and perfect a "successful pass." Thank goodness! Eighteen years or so gives us many opportunities to get it right. It never ceases to amaze me how forgiving children can be when parents humbly and honestly admit they blew it and then sincerely take the appropriate corrective action.

The key to raising financially responsible children is that *we must be what we want our children to become.* If we want them to become savers, we must save. If we want them to be honest in all matters, then we must be honest in all matters. If we want them to be patient and save up for what they want rather than demand to have it now and pay for it later, then that is how we must behave. We can preach only what we practice. If we want our children to become financially responsible adults, we must always provide a model, not just when we think they are watching. Never underestimate the power of a child's intuition and keen insight. What you do speaks so loudly your kids may not be able to hear what you say.

I believe that as soon as a child is given the opportunity to make choices he or she should be taught about money and then given the opportunity to make very simple and guided financial choices. For example, a four-year-old is old enough to make a choice between wearing the red or the blue shorts on some particular day or whether he or she would prefer orange or apple juice for breakfast. This is a good age to start teaching about money. Even a very young child quickly grasps the concept that money is valuable and buys things. This is the time to direct and channel healthy money attitudes.

Using all the visuals you can come up with, teach your child that some of his money should be saved. Use an appropriate bank, box, or envelope for the child's savings. Treat money as something with great dignity and value. Talk about saving for the future, about not spending all the money you have. Tell him or her simply how you save money in the bank. Talk about how you give away part of your money out of gratitude and thankfulness for all that you have.

Perhaps you will want to set up a program for the child where a portion of all of his/her money is saved for the long-term (college, perhaps?); a part is saved for the short-term (to buy a special toy); a part is given away (Sunday school, your local rescue mission, homeless support project, etc.), and part can be spent in any way the child wants. Whatever scheme you set up, stick to it. Make a big deal about it, too!

By starting early, you establish lifetime patterns and habits and also prevent yourself from becoming the "bad guy" in the future. The time will come that your children will get a case of the "I wants." They want everything in the store and without values and a financial program, you will soon become the mean parent who is constantly saying, "No! We just can't afford it."

By establishing a financial program for a child, many personal decisions come to rest upon their shoulders. Because they have money over which they have control, many spending decisions can revert to them. It is amazing how restrained a child can be even in the video arcade, when those quarters are their own!

As the child grows, so should the financial program. With age should come more responsibility. We established a program for our two boys which required them to save ten percent and give away 10 percent of their money. We set them up on "salary" because that term sounded mature and respectable. They had complete control over the eighty percent which remained and could do with it whatever they desired. The catch was they were responsible for a great deal of their own "costs" which expanded as their salary grew. They could make the choice, but a bad choice could result in a great deal of self-inflicted deprivation. We used the first day of each new school year as the day on which salary was increased and the responsibilities expanded.

In the beginning they were required to pay for a specific list of optional expenditures. This included video games, movies and outings with friends, birthday gifts for friends, things we felt were optional extras. By the time they graduated from high school, they were both paying for gasoline, driver's license fees, clothes (other than necessities), dates, school supplies—everything but their basic needs at home. They became such ardent savers, they each bought a car and paid for all maintenance. Our program instilled in them a keen sense of responsibility and independence. The best part has been the hassle-free years we've had because they have such a responsible attitude regarding money.

I believe the days are gone when the subject of money was considered inappropriate conversation because it was a topic just too private or intimate. On the contrary, your children should be allowed to see you striving to live beneath your means. They should learn about compounded interest. Show them a schedule of what will happen if they start saving $5 a week now. Teach them about options and security.

Your Freedom Account may become your very best visual teaching aid. Because it is separate from your day-to-day struggles, it should give your children a wonderful glimpse into your financial life without burdening them with adult-sized problems. Show them how you are planning for future expenses and saving for the family vacation. Impress upon them that we save the money first and then make the purchase. I am not in any way suggesting that children need to be aware of every aspect of your family's financial life. Pick and choose what is appropriate.

Let the world become your financial classroom. When children accompany you to the grocery store, teach them how to look for values. Tell them why you are using coupons or a calculator. Show them exactly how much money you have allotted for this trip and how important it is to stay below that amount. Don't stress deprivation, teach value and responsibility.

Consider your restaurant-tipping practices through the eyes of your child. Without a lesson, he may well think you are being extremely careless with your money by leaving some behind on the table. Show the kids how to determine how much of a tip to leave. What a great time to impart a lesson in generosity and gratitude.

And now to the subject of credit cards. Teach your kids about them. Remember, when a three- or four-year-old sees someone handing the cashier a credit card as payment, they think it is magic plastic. Think about it; you've taught them how valuable coins and currency are, but you use plastic. They get a wrong message imprinted on their brains. Tell them simply that when people use a credit card, they are promising to pay later, but they will be punished (tone that down if you desire, but that's how it feels to me) because they will have to pay much more money than if they would have waited until they could afford the item.

When you receive credit-card offerings in the mail, save them so you can teach your children about small print and at-times misleading advertisements. Teach them what "nothing down!" "deferred payments!" and "36 easy payments!" really means. You teach them about stranger dangers, now teach them about debt dangers. Make a simple diagram of how such a credit card could bring great financial peril upon the family by plunging them into terrible debt. Tell them about the feelings of entitlement and the false power a credit card can give.

Instill a healthy dose of fear about getting sucked into scams. Talk about addictions. Go ahead, tell them about me. I'll gladly be your negative model provided you tell the rest of the story, too. I don't think it would be wrong to tell them of your own struggles and mistakes. Let them in on your Rapid Debt-Repayment Plan. Allow them to celebrate each zero balance. Becoming accountable to your children might be a real healthy step. If you are a good teacher, you will be able to impart invaluable information, and the kids will come to their own responsible conclusions regarding unsecured credit.

Undoubtedly your children know there are things that you consider "family talk"—things that are to remain private within your own family. Your savings programs and investments may fall within this category, things we talk about among ourselves but keep private from the world. Sharing with your age-appropriate children about your payroll savings plan, 401K plan, insurance policies, etc. will become great lessons and conversation starters. Take advantage of them. Let your children know that when you must say "no" right now, it may well be for the reason that you have said "yes" to something more important like increased savings or a special Freedom Account item.

Never lose track of your objective of passing on the baton of financial responsibility. Keep your eye on the goal of raising children who are self-reliant, children who know the joy of saving and giving as well as consuming.

. . . I allowed my 15-year-old to take the money she got for her birthday and let her loose in the local mall alone, shopping for school clothes. I added the same amount of money I'd spent on my younger daughter's clothes to the money she had. When I dropped her off I gave her a specific time I would pick her up. Upon returning to retrieve her, the first words out of her mouth were, "I can't believe the prices of jeans here! Boy, this is highway robbery! So I didn't buy any jeans." What a change! When "MOM" was there with her charge cards the sky was the limit. Wow! What a change when she had to pull money from her wallet!

Carol Sue

CHAPTER 15

Difficult Situations

No-Fault Financial Problems

Not everyone's financial situation is a result of poor money management. Perhaps you are suffering because of huge medical bills not covered by insurance. Maybe you are a single parent trying to survive on a below-poverty level income. My recommendation is that you follow the principles of the Money Makeover as far as they may be possible, and then not be ashamed to seek assistance from outside sources. In this country there are thousands of charitable organizations and governmental agencies which might be able to help you. Of course your best tactic is still to find new ways to cut expenses.

Self-employment

If you look to commission sales or other forms of self-employment as your sole source of income, the word "roller coaster" probably brings more to mind than a large steel edifice at Six Flags Over Somewhere. And I would not be surprised if because of your status you have not dismissed most of what you have read thus far as inapplicable to your situation.

Having been self-employed most of my working years, I know exactly the justifications for being unable to plan ahead or stick with a plan.

The majority of those who fall into the irregular income category live in constant uncertainty. Some months can produce absolutely no income, then a deal closes or a big account comes through resulting in a good-sized check which usually is applied in its entirety to catching up. During those particularly wonderful months the entitlement mentality kicks in, demanding that something extravagant be purchased. Somehow when the big deal closes we forget about the lean months and the fact that there may be many more ahead.

"Feast or famine" sums it up. For many, at least in the beginning, self-employment is survival on a daily basis. "Self-employeds" usually conclude it is impossible to come up with any kind of reasonable spending plan or to live within one's means when the means are so unpredictable. But this is wrong!

Commissioned salespersons, freelancers as well as small business owners, make a huge mistake when they fail to become their own strict and unbending employer. Those of us in this position must wear two different hats—that of employer and employee.

As the employee you need to determine honestly what is the lowest reasonable amount you can accept from yourself, the employer, as monthly compensation. Now that's a new twist. Usually self-employeds ask, "what is the largest amount I can possibly pull out of this business every month?" Let's say, for example, that your rock-bottom absolutely minimum figure is $3,000 a month, based upon your Monthly Spending Plan. You may intend to bring $10 million into the business this year, but determining your reasonable monthly requirements has nothing to do with that. As your employer you must determine if the "business" (this applies to commissioned sales people, too, who should see themselves as self-employed) is able to commit to this $3,000 monthly salary for its favorite "employee." Let's assume that it can.

Next you must open another checking account. If you are a typical small business owner, you take varying sums of money (depending upon current need or availability) directly from the business account and deposit them into your personal checking account. The amount probably fluctuates greatly from month to month. As a freelance artist or commissioned salesperson you have been used to depositing your commission checks or payments directly into your personal account. This is a problem!

By opening another checking account, you will be

able to take control. Example: You receive a $10,000 commission check in January, nothing in February, nothing in March; in April you receive five checks, $550, $1,200, $3,000 and $850. Not so bad. That's $15,600 for four months which should more than cover your expenses of $3,000 a month. The problem is in January you might have had to play catch-up on all of the holiday bills which you couldn't pay because December was a "dry" month. And then there were all of those great sales and it felt like you had extra money so you splurged a bit here and there. Along comes February and March and no income. The personal checking account is depleted, the credit cards are called into action, and it's desperation time until April. The $5,600 received in April barely gets you caught up, and so goes the ride on the roller coaster.

With the new checking account method here is what would happen: the January $10,000 check would *not* be deposited into the regular checking account. Instead it would go into the holding account (or whatever you want to call it). You would become a very strict and stern employer and guard this account as any good employer or business owner would. On "payday," that is, a predetermined day that you pay yourself each month, you write yourself, the employee, a paycheck for $3,000 —*regardless of the balance in that account*. After all, as your own employee you can't expect a raise every month. It's $3,000 (or whatever the amount you have previously negotiated with yourself) on payday and that's it. On February 1 you write yourself a $3,000 paycheck. On March 1 you write yourself a $3,000 paycheck. On April 1 you deposit the $5,600 and write yourself a $3,000 paycheck and so on each month.

If your self-employment career is sufficient to support you and your family, you should not have to worry. The income flowing into the holding account should exceed the paychecks. As the holding account becomes healthy, there will be additional funds to carry you through lean times. When things are going well and there are sufficient reserves, you might even consider sitting down with yourself to negotiate a raise, but remember to think this through. Weigh the pros and cons. Consider the position of the prudent employer and the needy employee.

The self-employed's major problem is the temptation to live it up when a big check comes in. After all, surely there's a bigger and better deal just around the corner which will take care of the future. It looks and feels like you're living within your means, but don't be deceived. Your success as a self-employed person lies in your ability to discipline yourself and be a fair but strict employer and at the same time a grateful, restrained employee.

Negotiating with creditors

What happens when one's financial situation becomes so dire that even after doing everything we've discussed (keeping impeccable spending records, setting up a Freedom Account, cutting expenses to rock bottom, and incurring no new debt) ends still don't meet? When there's nothing left to cut, no hope of increasing income and no more assets to liquidate?

What follows are suggestions for only the most desperate situations. Unless you have honestly tried every tactic to bring your spending in line with your income and kept impeccable spending records for at least four months you probably shouldn't even be reading this.

This is for those very serious situations in which bankruptcy seems like the best alternative, but you are willing to try one last possibility.

Look at your list of debts. There's no doubt they are what's killing you. Minimum monthly payments may exceed your total income. By now these creditors are sick of hearing your stories and promises and you're just as sick of hearing their threats. Perhaps you've been avoiding their calls, allowing their collection tactics to ruin your day and throw you into depression.

Look back at your Monthly Spending Plan. Ignoring your Freedom Account and Rapid Debt-Repayment Plan, what is the total of your *essential* monthly expenses? (I assume you have cut this to the bare bone, and that this number represents only your basic needs.) When you deduct these expenses from your average monthly income, how much is left? If it isn't enough to pay your minimum monthly debt payments, how close is it? To find out, divide the amount of money left over after paying for essential monthly expenses by the total of your minimum monthly debt payments. That will give you a percentage. Let's say for illustration purposes it is 60 percent. You can't pay 100 percent of your monthly payments on your debts, but you can pay 60 percent.

I am not about to propose that any of your creditors waive payments. I'm suggesting that given the right set of circumstances your creditors *might* be willing to work with you to renegotiate the terms of your pay back. But you must approach them in a very mature, sincere, and responsible manner, and you may have to ask forgiveness for your past behavior.

First, you need to look deeply into your heart. Are you willing to keep whatever promise you make to your creditors? If you cannot embrace integrity as part of your new makeover, you will not succeed.

None of this is going to be easy. I hate confrontations, you probably do, too. My knees get weak and my voice trembles when I have to make difficult phone calls. I find writing letters to be easier, but not always as effective.

Look at your Rapid Debt-Repayment Plan. First, take each of your minimum monthly debt payments and multiply by the percentage you can pay. Next contact each of your creditors and tell them: I have a real financial problem. I don't want to declare bankruptcy. I've entered into a financial recovery program. I have come up with a plan that I am dedicated to working with and a repayment plan to which I am committed. I do not want you to suffer, and I am determined to pay back every single cent I owe you. I intend to pay you 60 percent (or the percentage you have determined) of my current monthly payment. I promise to pay you the same amount every month even if my required minimum payment drops. I need your help.

On the following page is a letter which would be appropriate to send to each of your creditors. Feel free to use it verbatim on one condition: You must be willing to carry through and make every promised payment. This is a serious letter and should not be used without a great deal of thought.

The letter ends with an "assumptive close." You are asking for a favor and are assuming it will be granted and as such you are acting as if it has been accepted. You must enclose a check or money order to demonstrate your good faith and commitment.

Creditor Name
Creditor Address
Date

RE: Account _____

Gentlemen,

I (or we) am writing to you about my account
as referenced above. I deeply regret that I
have fallen behind and have failed to abide by
the terms of our agreement. I want you to
know that I am committed to full repayment in
the amount of $_____.

I have recently undertaken a financial
recovery program and have assessed my
financial situation. As a result, I have created
a full repayment plan. I am doing everything I
possibly can to avoid filing for bankruptcy.

Your account, unfortunately, is only one of the
many that I owe; my total debt is $_____
with monthly payments totaling $_____.
You can understand that my present net
monthly income of $_____, less
drastically reduced living expenses of rent,
food, utilities, etc., does not leave funds
sufficient to pay even the minimum monthly
payments to which I agreed.

Enclosed please find my check in the amount
of $_____ which represents the amount I
will be able to pay each month on my account
for the next six months. At that time my
situation will be reviewed. Hopefully the
payments will be increased regularly to allow

for total repayment at the earliest possible date.

I respectfully request that the interest rate you are charging be reduced so that a greater portion of my payment will go toward principal reduction. Further, I request that during this recovery period when you are accepting these lower payments you not report this account as late to the credit bureaus as long as I make these new payments on time.

My financial recovery program projects that I will be completely debt-free within _____ years.

I look forward to learning that you have processed this payment in acceptance of my requests. If however, you are unwilling to work with me as outlined above kindly return the enclosed payment so that I can send an additional payment to another of my creditors who has agreed.

Thank you in advance for your cooperation.

Sincerely,

Hopefully, each check or money order enclosed with these letters to your creditors will be cashed. In my opinion the fact that the payment was accepted indicates the creditor has accepted your offer. You may continue to receive phone calls, but receive them courteously.

Keep your recovery program and your commitment to full repayment uppermost in your mind. Whatever you do, don't miss a single payment and don't be late with your payments. After six months, contact your creditors again. Let them know how the plan is going and tell them if you will be able to increase the payment.

Some people have had great success with this approach, while others have encountered creditors who don't want anything to do with renegotiating. But don't let one "no" defeat you. Send that creditor another letter in a week or two. Change the words, but don't change the message. Send it to the supervisor or the president of the company with an explanation that your offer has been turned down but you are sure management will rethink this response. Be courteous but persistent, persistent, persistent.

Bankruptcy

Some financial situations are beyond repair. In these situations there are few choices besides filing for bankruptcy. While bankruptcy can offer a fresh start for some, it can also turn out to be a 10-year mistake if filed in haste or without sufficient cause.

Do not think about filing for bankruptcy until all other options have been considered and exhausted. Once you have filed it will be nearly impossible to get credit, rent a home or apartment, travel or write checks for instance. A financial leper is how many who have taken such a drastic step describe themselves. Don't believe anyone who tries to convince you this step will be easy or a joyful way to start over.

It might be advisable to contact Consumer Credit Counseling Services before filing bankruptcy just to get a second opinion. You may find you have an alternative.

If you decide to file, shop for a reasonably priced bankruptcy lawyer who will explain the pros and cons. I would be suspicious of anyone who tried to convince me it was all good and very easy.

Many people who go through a bankruptcy find a welcomed sense of relief but the inevitable emotional toll should not be underrated. Bankruptcy will be on your record for life. Accept that. Even though it may drop off your credit report in ten years, you will still have to answer truthfully whenever you purchase real estate or engage in other major transactions and are asked, "Have you ever filed for bankruptcy protection?"

I hope that you will learn from your past experience and not go back to living beyond your means. Believe it or not, after filing for bankruptcy you will become what some creditors consider a good risk. They will try to load you up with new debt because they know you can't file again for bankruptcy for a number of years.

Your fresh start should include living by the principles of this Money Makeover. They will help you get started on the right foot, stay focused and stay out of trouble.

During these difficult times take care of your relationships. Don't underestimate the impact of bankruptcy on your spouse and children, both as part of the family and individually. You will all more than likely need to go through the stages of anger, guilt, and grief. In some ways it will be like facing a death.

But after the rain comes sunshine. There is a new tomorrow so "pick yourself up, dust yourself off and start all over again."

. . . there I was, a very young single mother lacking direction, without child support, and battling depression. I took my daughter and moved to another city hoping to escape an abusive ex-husband.

I lived on credit as long as I could and ran up such a mess I figured my only solution was to file for bankruptcy. I saw this as a way to wipe the slate clean and treated the whole mess as part of the past. I figured I was entitled to a fresh start.

I found a way to get a whole new identity and a new set of credit cards and did I ever use them! I thrived on the instant gratification they offered. Eventually I started my own business which really sped up my debt-making abilities. I worshipped money and just couldn't get enough of it. It was my anesthetic of choice and deadened all the pain I was facing in my personal life. At one point I had 10 separate checking accounts.

I began buying real estate. At last I had found my niche and no one was more surprised than I at my newfound business success. I learned to use every leveraging tactic known to the business world to mortgage myself into oblivion. I became a magician at juggling accounts, payments, and refinancing.

During the height of my career as a real estate tycoon, I married a wonderful man. He married an image, and believe me—I had created some image! Within a very short period of time after we were married, I could no longer keep the juggling act up and my house of cards crashed. My new husband got to meet the real me.

We had no choice but to file for bankruptcy. I cannot describe the humiliation, the pain—the shame and the disgrace of going through bankruptcy again, but this time dragging my new husband along with me. I hurt him, I hurt many other people, and I destroyed valued friendships.

The difference this time, however, is that we did not attempt to fix things by ourselves. I've taken full responsibility for what I've done and am willing to learn from the mistakes of the past. We no longer live to keep up an image. By turning our lives over to the control of God and applying sound financial principles to our lives we have been able to pick up the broken pieces and put things back together. We have begun a formal savings plan, we pay our bills on time, and we've been able to buy a home. My priorities have completely changed as I am learning to discern what is important and what is not.

Filing for bankruptcy twice is something that I am so ashamed of. However, in some odd way I am learning to be thankful for that, too, because as a result I am finally learning how to be financially responsible and content.

Hydee

CHAPTER 16

It's Never Too Late

I've never written or told a living soul of our predicament as I am embarrassed. At our age, most retirees are living comfortably on their assets. But we are not. We are in our seventies and eighties and live on our social security and a small pension. We live from one month to the next and it is a struggle. We always hoped to start saving someday. We need to see if we can better ourselves but I think it's too late.

Yes, we do have credit cards—six of them representing about $4,000 in debt. Our bills get paid on time, because even if we have to take it out of our grocery allowance they get paid first.

Our debt may not seem large to some, but at our age it seems like millions. Neither of us can work anymore so we feel trapped . . .

Betty

It is never too late to become what you might have been. No matter in which season of life you find yourself it is not too late to get started with your own Money Makeover. It's never too late to start saving, to become filled with the spirit of generosity, or to make necessary adjustments to rein in your spending.

It's not too late to begin listening carefully to the quietest tickings of your heart. It's not too late to start fulfilling your dreams.

Becoming who you want to be may entail a giant leap of faith. It may mean believing that you can hang up a shingle and make a living by following your dreams. It may mean casting yourself as the hero of your own story.

I allowed my eyes to get me into a lot of financial trouble. I saw nice things and I wanted them. I wanted others to see me as prosperous and well-to-do. I didn't practice restraint, and did everything I could to have things "right now". The rest is history.

My failure to see the invisible was my undoing. I was so busy amassing what I could see, I completely ignored the things I couldn't. I didn't see the miracle of compounded interest, I didn't see what it was doing to me as my foe nor what it could have done for me had I embraced it as a friend. I failed to see the joy and happiness I was stealing from my future.

But it was not too late. I realized that unless I changed the direction I was going I would surely end up where I was headed. I turned around. And you can too.

As you begin the rest of your life with your new

Money Makeover, look for the invisible. Embrace joy, choose happiness, and hold fast to those intangibles which cannot be taken from you.

Don't become a compulsive hoarder or a compulsive spender. Save, give, plan, anticipate, and then live life to its fullest!

And please, don't deny yourself the simple pleasures in life. Just make sure that if they have a price tag you pay for them with CASH!

"You give PEACE to all who love your laws."
Psa. 119:165

Resources

Counseling

Debtors Anonymous. If you have a problem with debting, you may wish to check them out. DA is a 12-Step Program which operates very much like Alcoholics Anonymous. They use the same guidelines and principles. To locate a group in your area you may call (212) 642-8222 or write: Debtors Anonymous, General Service Board, P.O. Box 411, Grand Central Station, New York, NY 10163-0400.

National Foundation for Consumer Credit. Consumer Credit Counseling (CCCS) provides low-cost or free assistance to consumers who are having trouble paying their bills. To find the office in your area call 1-800-388-CCCS. You will be referred to one of the more than 600 local offices.

Overspenders Anonymous. If you have a problem controlling your spending, this 12-Step Program may be for you. Check the white pages of your telephone book to find out if there is a group in your area.

Consumer Fresh Start. This is a group for people who have declared bankruptcy. They provide counseling, support, and other benefits. Call them at (815) 875-4078 or write: 217 N. Church St., Princeton, IL 61356.

Books & Newsletters

Cutting Expenses

52 Ways to Stretch a Buck, Kenny Luck, Thomas Nelson Publishers.

1001 Ways to Cut Your Expenses, Jonathan D. Pond, Dell Publishers.

The Best of Cheapskate Monthly, Simple Tips for Living Lean in the 90s, Mary Hunt, St. Martin's Press.

Cheaper and Better, Homemade Alternatives to Storebought Goods, Nancy Birnes, Harper & Row.

Cheapskate Monthly, newsletter, P.O. Box 2135, Paramount, CA 90723-8135. Published monthly. (See following page for special offer.)

Cut Your Bills in Half, the Editors of Rodale Press.

Cut Your Spending in Half, How to Pay the Lowest Price for Everything Without Settling for Less, the Editors of Rodale Press, distributed by St. Martin's Press.

Eat Well for $50 a Week, Rhonda Barfield, Lilac Publishing, P.O. Box 665, St. Charles, MO 63302-0655.

The Penny Pincher's Almanac, Handbook for Modern Frugality, Hundreds of Simple Ways to Spend Less and Get More, Dean King and the Editors of *The Penny Pincher's Almanac.*

Penny Pinching, How to Lower Your Everyday Expenses Without Lowering Your Standard of Living, Lee and Barbara Simmons, Bantam Books.

Saving Money Any Way You Can, Mike Yorkey, Servant Publications, 1-800-486-8505.

Planning and Budgeting

The Family Budget Workbook, Gaining Control of Your Personal Finances, Larry Burkett, Moody Press.

Get Rich Slow, the Truth (not the hype) About What to do With Your Money and Why, Tama McAleese, Career Press, 1-800-CAREER-1.

How to Get Out of Debt, Stay Out of Debt and Live Prosperously, Jerrold Mundis, Bantam Books.

Make Your Paycheck Last: The Complete Step by Step Guide to Personal and Family Financial Success, Harold Moe, Career Press, 1-800-CAREER-1.

The Money Drunk, 90 Days to Financial Freedom, Mark Bryan and Julia Cameron, Ballantine Books.

Saving and Investing

Guide to Understanding Money & Investing, Morris and Siegel, *The Wall Street Journal* and Lightbulb Press, distributed by Simon & Schuster.

How to Invest $50–$5,000, Nancy Dunnan, Harper Perennial.

Straight Talk About Mutual Funds, Dian Vujovich, McGraw-Hill.

What is Cheapskate Monthly?

Cheapskate Monthly is an eight-page newsletter published twelve times a year, dedicated to helping those who are struggling to live within their means find practical and realistic methods and solutions to their financial problems. *Cheapskate Monthly* provides hope, encouragement, inspiration, and motivation to individuals who are committed to financially responsible and debt-free living and provides the highest quality information and resources possible in a format exclusive of paid advertising. You will find *Cheapskate Monthly* filled with tips, humor, and just plain great information to help you stretch those dollars 'til they scream!

Ask for Mary Hunt's first <u>book</u> . . .

The Best of Cheapskate Monthly
Simple Tips for Living Lean in the '90s

at your favorite bookstore!
ISBN 0-312-95093-4
Published by
St. Martin's Paperbacks

"So affordable it will easily fit within your
Spending Plan!"

"Her straightforward advice ranges on subjects from
coupons and discount shopping to insurance policies
. . . Hunt's upbeat attitude doesn't come across as a
lecture and she makes it clear she's not denying
herself simple pleasures."—*Los Angeles Times*

"Hunt has become so competent at pinching pennies
that she teaches others the fine art through
Cheapskate Monthly."—*Business Week*